編者的話

　　「學科能力測驗」是「指定科目考試」的前哨站，雖然難度較「指考」低，但是考試內容以及成績，仍然非常具有參考價值，而且「學測」考得好的同學，還可以甄選入學的方式，比別人早一步進入理想的大學，提前放暑假。

　　為了協助考生以最有效率的方式準備大學入學考試，我們特別蒐集了 102 年度「學測」各科試題，包括英文、數學、社會、自然和國文，做成「**102 年學科能力測驗各科試題詳解**」，書後並附有大考中心所公佈的各科選擇題答案、成績統計表，以及國文、英文兩科非選擇題閱卷評分原則說明。另外，在英文科詳解後面，還附上了英文試題修正意見及英文考科選文出處，讀者可利用空檔時間，上網瀏覽那些網站，增進自己的課外知識，並了解出題方向。

　　這本書的完成，要感謝各科名師全力協助解題：

　英文 / 謝靜芳老師・蔡琇瑩老師・林工富老師
　　　　蔡世偉老師・李冠勳老師・周敬濤老師
　　　　葉哲榮老師
　　　　美籍老師 Laura E. Stewart
　　　　　　　　　Christain A. Brieske

　數學 / 劉駿豪老師
　社會 / 李　曄老師・王念平老師・李　易老師
　國文 / 李雅清老師
　自然 / 林清華老師・邱炳華老師・游　夏老師
　　　　柯　舜老師

　　本書編校製作過程嚴謹，但仍恐有缺失之處，尚祈各界先進不吝指正。

劉　毅

CONTENTS

102 年大學入學學科能力測驗試題
英文考科

第壹部分：單選題（占 72 分）

一、詞彙（占 15 分）

說明：第 1 題至第 15 題，每題有 4 個選項，其中只有一個是正確或最適當的選項，請畫記在答案卡之「選擇題答案區」。各題答對者，得 1 分；答錯、未作答或畫記多於一個選項者，該題以零分計算。

1. It rained so hard yesterday that the baseball game had to be _____ until next Saturday.
   (A) surrendered　　(B) postponed　　(C) abandoned　　(D) opposed

2. As more people rely on the Internet for information, it has _____ newspapers as the most important source of news.
   (A) distributed　　(B) subtracted　　(C) replaced　　(D) transferred

3. Having saved enough money, Joy _____ two trips for this summer vacation, one to France and the other to Australia.
   (A) booked　　(B) observed　　(C) enclosed　　(D) deposited

4. Since I do not fully understand your proposal, I am not in the position to make any _____ on it.
   (A) difference　　(B) solution　　(C) demand　　(D) comment

5. Betty was _____ to accept her friend's suggestion because she thought she could come up with a better idea herself.
   (A) tolerable　　(B) sensitive　　(C) reluctant　　(D) modest

6. The bank tries its best to attract more customers. Its staff members are always available to provide _____ service.
   (A) singular　　(B) prompt　　(C) expensive　　(D) probable

7. John's part-time experience at the cafeteria is good _____ for running his own restaurant.
   (A) preparation   (B) recognition (C) formation   (D) calculation

8. Women's fashions are _____ changing: One season they may favor pantsuits, but the next season they may prefer miniskirts.
   (A) lately   (B) shortly   (C) relatively   (D) constantly

9. Standing on the seashore, we saw a _____ of seagulls flying over the ocean before they glided down and settled on the water.
   (A) pack   (B) flock   (C) herd   (D) school

10. The book is not only informative but also _____, making me laugh and feel relaxed while reading it.
    (A) understanding (B) infecting   (C) entertaining (D) annoying

11. After working in front of my computer for the entire day, my neck and shoulders got so _____ that I couldn't even turn my head.
    (A) dense   (B) harsh   (C) stiff   (D) concrete

12. Getting a flu shot before the start of flu season gives our body a chance to build up protection against the _____ that could make us sick.
    (A) poison   (B) misery   (C) leak   (D) virus

13. The kingdom began to _____ after the death of its ruler, and was soon taken over by a neighboring country.
    (A) collapse   (B) dismiss   (C) rebel   (D) withdraw

14. Though Kevin failed in last year's singing contest, he did not feel _____. This year he practiced day and night and finally won first place in the competition.
    (A) relieved   (B) suspected   (C) discounted   (D) frustrated

15. Emma and Joe are looking for a live-in babysitter for their three-year-old twins, _____ one who knows how to cook.
    (A) initially   (B) apparently   (C) preferably   (D) considerably

二、綜合測驗（占 15 分）

說明： 第 16 題至第 30 題，每題一個空格，請依文意選出最適當的一個選項，請畫記在答案卡之「選擇題答案區」。各題答對者，得 1 分；答錯、未作答或畫記多於一個選項者，該題以零分計算。

An area code is a section of a telephone number which generally represents the geographical area that the phone receiving the call is based in. It is the two or three digits just before the local number. If the number ___16___ is in the same area as the number making the call, an area code usually doesn't need to be dialed. The local number, ___17___ , must always be dialed in its entirety.

The area code was introduced in the United States in 1947. It was created ___18___ the format of XYX, with X being any number between 2-9 and Y being either 1 or 0. Cities and areas with higher populations would have a smaller first and third digit, and 1 as the center digit. New York, being the largest city in the United States, was ___19___ the 212 area code, followed by Los Angeles at 213.

In countries other than the United States and Canada, the area code generally determines the ___20___ of a call. Calls within an area code and often a small group of neighboring area codes are normally charged at a lower rate than outside the area code.

16. (A) calling   (B) being called
    (C) having called   (D) has been calling
17. (A) in fact   (B) to illustrate
    (C) at the same time   (D) on the other hand
18. (A) for   (B) as   (C) by   (D) in
19. (A) reserved   (B) assigned   (C) represented   (D) assembled
20. (A) cost   (B) format   (C) quality   (D) distance

For coin collectors who invest money in coins, the value of a coin is determined by various factors. First, scarcity is a major determinant. ___21___ a coin is, the more it is worth. Note, however, that rarity has little to do with the ___22___ of a coin. Many thousand-year-old coins often sell for no more than a few dollars because there are a lot of them around, ___23___ a 1913 Liberty Head Nickel may sell for over one million US dollars because there are only five in existence. Furthermore, the demand for a particular coin will also ___24___ influence coin values. Some coins may command higher prices because they are more popular with collectors. For example, a 1798 dime is much rarer than a 1916 dime, but the ___25___ sells for significantly more, simply because many more people collect early 20th century dimes than dimes from the 1700s.

21. (A) Rare as   (B) The rare   (C) Rarest   (D) The rarer
22. (A) age   (B) shape   (C) size   (D) weight
23. (A) since   (B) while   (C) whether   (D) if
24. (A) merely   (B) hardly   (C) greatly   (D) roughly
25. (A) older   (B) better   (C) latter   (D) bigger

French psychologist Alfred Binet (1859-1911) took a different approach from most other psychologists of his day: He was interested in the workings of the ___26___ mind rather than the nature of mental illness. He wanted to find a way to measure the ability to think and reason, apart from education in any particular field. In 1905 he developed a test in which he ___27___ children do tasks such as follow commands, copy patterns, name objects, and put things in order or arrange them properly. He later created a standard of measuring children's intelligence ___28___ the data he had collected from the French children he studied. If 70 percent of 8-year-olds could pass a particular test, then ___29___ on the test represented an 8-year-old's level of intelligence. From Binet's work, the phrase "intelligence quotient" ("IQ") entered the English vocabulary. The IQ is the ratio of "mental age" to chronological age times 100, with 100 ___30___ the average. So, an 8-year-old who passes the 10-year-old's test would have an IQ of 10/8 times 100, or 125.

26. (A) contrary   (B) normal   (C) detective   (D) mutual
27. (A) had   (B) kept   (C) wanted   (D) asked
28. (A) composed of   (B) based on
     (C) resulting in   (D) fighting against
29. (A) success   (B) objection   (C) agreement   (D) discovery
30. (A) is   (B) are   (C) been   (D) being

三、文意選填（占 10 分）

說明： 第 31 題至第 40 題，每題一個空格，請依文意在文章後所提供的 (A) 到
(J) 選項中分別選出最適當者，並將其英文字母代號畫記在答案卡之「選
擇題答案區」。各題答對者，得 1 分；答錯、未作答或畫記多於一個選
項者，該題以零分計算。

     Often called "rainforests of the sea," coral reefs provide a home for 25% of all species in the ocean. They are stony structures full of dark hideaways where fish and sea animals can lay their eggs and ___31___ from predators. Without these underwater "apartment houses," there would be fewer fish in the ocean. Some species might even become ___32___ or disappear completely.

     There are thousands of reefs in the world; ___33___, however, they are now in serious danger. More than one-third are in such bad shape that they could die within ten years. Many might not even ___34___ that long! Scientists are working hard to find out what leads to this destruction. There are still a lot of questions unanswered, but three main causes have been ___35___.

     The first cause is pollution on land. The pollutants run with rainwater into rivers and streams, which ___36___ the poisons into the ocean. Chemicals from the poisons kill reefs or make them weak, so they have less ___37___ to diseases.

Global warming is another reason. Higher ocean temperatures kill the important food source for the coral—the algae, the tiny greenish-gold water plants that live on coral. When the algae die, the coral loses its color and it also dies ___38___. This process, known as "coral bleaching," has happened more and more frequently in recent years.

The last factor contributing to the ___39___ of coral reefs is people. People sometimes crash into reefs with their boats or drop anchors on them, breaking off large chunks of coral. Divers who walk on reefs can also do serious damage. Moreover, some people even break coral off to collect for ___40___ since it is so colorful and pretty.

How can we help the reefs? We need to learn more about them and work together to stop the activities that may threaten their existence.

(A) resistance　　(B) identified　　(C) last　　　　　(D) escape
(E) sadly　　　　 (F) eventually　 (G) disappearance　(H) souvenirs
(I) endangered　 (J) carry

四、閱讀測驗（占 32 分）

說明： 第 41 題至第 56 題，每題請分別根據各篇文章之文意選出最適當的一個
選項，請畫記在答案卡之「選擇題答案區」。各題答對者，得 2 分；答
錯、未作答或畫記多於一個選項者，該題以零分計算。

第 41 至 44 題為題組

The Swiss army knife is a popular device that is recognized all over the world. In Switzerland, there is a saying that every good Swiss citizen has one in his or her pocket. But the knife had humble beginnings.

In the late nineteenth century, the Swiss army issued its soldiers a gun that required a special screwdriver to dismantle and clean it. At the same time, canned food was becoming common in the army. Swiss generals decided to issue each soldier a standard knife to serve both as a screwdriver and a can opener.

It was a lifesaver for Swiss knife makers, who were struggling to compete with cheaper German imports. In 1884, Carl Elsener, head of the Swiss knife manufacturer Victorinox, seized that opportunity with both hands, and designed a soldier's knife that the army loved. It was a simple knife with one big blade, a can opener, and a screwdriver.

A few years after the soldier's knife was issued, the "Schweizer Offizier Messer," or Swiss Officer's Knife, came on the market. Interestingly, the Officer's Knife was never given to those serving in the army. The Swiss military purchasers considered the new model with a corkscrew for opening wine not "essential for survival," so officers had to buy this new model by themselves. But its special multi-functional design later launched the knife as a global brand. After the Second World War, a great number of American soldiers were stationed in Europe. And as they could buy the Swiss army knife at shops on military bases, they bought huge quantities of them. However, it seems that "Schweizer Offizier Messer" was too difficult for them to say, so they just called it the Swiss army knife, and that is the name it is now known by all over the world.

41. What is the main purpose of the passage?
    (A) To explain the origin of the Swiss army knife.
    (B) To introduce the functions of the Swiss army knife.
    (C) To emphasize the importance of the Swiss army knife.
    (D) To tell a story about the designer of the Swiss army knife.

42. What does "**It**" in the third paragraph refer to?
    (A) The Swiss army needed a knife for every soldier.
    (B) Every good Swiss citizen had a knife in his pocket.
    (C) Swiss knives were competing with imported knives.
    (D) Canned food was becoming popular in the Swiss army.

43. Why didn't the Swiss army purchase the Swiss Officer's Knife?
    (A) The design of the knife was too simple.
    (B) The knife was sold out to American soldiers.
    (C) The army had no budget to make the purchase.
    (D) The new design was not considered necessary for officers to own.

44. Who gave the name "the Swiss army knife" to the knife discussed in the passage?
    (A) Carl Elsener.   (B) Swiss generals.
    (C) American soldiers.   (D) German businessmen.

第 45 至 48 題為題組

　　Space is where our future is—trips to the Moon, Mars and beyond. Most people would think that aside from comets and stars there is little else out there. But, since our space journey started we have left so much trash there that scientists are now concerned that if we don't clean it up, we may all be in mortal danger.

　　The first piece of space junk was created in 1964, when the American satellite Vanguard I stopped operating and lost its connection with the ground center. However, since it kept orbiting around the Earth without any consequences, scientists became increasingly comfortable abandoning things that no longer served any useful purpose in space.

　　It is estimated that there are currently over 500,000 pieces of man-made trash orbiting the Earth at speeds of up to 17,500 miles per hour. The junk varies from tiny pieces of paint chipped off rockets to cameras, huge fuel tanks, and even odd items like the million-dollar tool kit that astronaut Heidemarie Stefanyshyn-Piper lost during a spacewalk.

　　The major problem with the space trash is that it may hit working satellites and damage traveling spacecraft. Moreover, pieces of junk may collide with each other and break into fragments which fall back to the Earth. To avoid this, scientists have devised several ways for clearing the sky. Ground stations have been built to monitor larger pieces of space trash to prevent them from crashing into working satellites or space shuttles. Future plans include a cooperative effort among many nations to stop littering in space and to clean up the trash already there.

45. What was the first piece of man-made space trash?
(A) A camera.　　　　　(B) A tool kit.
(C) A fuel tank.　　　　(D) A broken satellite.

46. Why were scientists **NOT** concerned about space trash in the beginning?
(A) It no longer served any useful purpose.
(B) It was millions of miles away from the Earth.
(C) It did not cause any problems.
(D) It was regarded as similar to comets and stars.

47. Which of the following statements is true about space junk?
(A) It is huge, heavy machines.
(B) It never changes position.
(C) It floats slowly around the Earth.
(D) It may cause problems for space shuttles.

48. What has been done about the space trash problem?
(A) Scientists have cleaned up most of the trash.
(B) Large pieces of space trash are being closely watched.
(C) Many nations have worked together to stop polluting space.
(D) Ground stations are built to help store the trash properly in space.

第 49 至 52 題為題組

An alcohol breath test (ABT) is often used by the police to find out whether a person is drunk while driving. In the United States, the legal blood alcohol limit is 0.08% for people aged 21 years or older, while people under 21 are not allowed to drive a car with any level of alcohol in their body. A "positive" test result, a result over the legal limit, allows the police to arrest the driver. However, many people who tested positive on the test have claimed that they only drank a "non-alcoholic" energy drink. Can one of these energy drinks really cause someone to test positive on an ABT? Researchers in Missouri set up an experiment to find out.

First, the amount of alcohol in 27 different popular energy drinks was measured. All but one had an alcohol level greater than 0.005%. In nine of the 27 drinks, the alcohol level was at least 0.096%. The scientists then investigated the possibility that these small levels of alcohol could be detected by an ABT. They asked test subjects to drink a full can or bottle of an energy drink and then gave each subject an ABT one minute and 15 minutes after the drink was finished.

For 11 of the 27 energy drinks, the ABT did detect the presence of alcohol if the test was given within one minute after the drink was taken. However, alcohol could not be detected for any of the drinks if the test was given 15 minutes after the drink was consumed. This shows that when the test is taken plays a crucial role in the test result. The sooner the test is conducted after the consumption of these drinks, the more likely a positive alcohol reading will be obtained.

49. For a person who just turned 20, what is the legal alcohol level allowed while driving in the US?
(A) 0.000%.　　(B) 0.005%.　　(C) 0.080%.　　(D) 0.096%.

50. What is the purpose of the Missouri experiment?
(A) To introduce a new method of calculating blood alcohol levels.
(B) To discover the relation between energy drinks and ABT test results.
(C) To warn about the dangers of drinking energy drinks mixed with alcohol.
(D) To challenge the current legal alcohol limit for drivers in the United States.

51. What were the participants of the experiment asked to do after they finished their energy drink?
    (A) To line up in the laboratory.
    (B) To recall the drink brands.
    (C) To take an alcohol breath test.
    (D) To check their breath for freshness.

52. What is the most important factor that affects the ABT test result for energy drink consumers?
    (A) The age of the person who takes the test.
    (B) The place where the test is given.
    (C) The equipment that the test uses.
    (D) The time when the test is taken.

第 53 至 56 題為題組

The majority of Indian women wear a red dot between their eyebrows. While it is generally taken as an indicator of their marital status, the practice is primarily related to the Hindu religion. The dot goes by different names in different Hindi dialects, and "bindi" is the one that is most commonly known. Traditionally, the dot carries no gender restriction: Men as well as women wear it. However, the tradition of men wearing it has faded in recent times, so nowadays we see a lot more women than men wearing one.

The position of the bindi is standard: center of the forehead, close to the eyebrows. It represents a third, or inner eye. Hindu tradition holds that all people have three eyes: The two outer ones are used for seeing the outside world, and the third one is there to focus inward toward God. As such, the dot signifies piety and serves as a constant reminder to keep God in the front of a believer's thoughts.

Red is the traditional color of the dot. It is said that in ancient times a man would place a drop of blood between his wife's eyes to seal their marriage. According to Hindu beliefs, the color red is believed to bring good fortune to the married couple. Today, people go with different colors depending upon their preferences. Women often wear dots that match the color of their clothes. Decorative or sticker bindis come in all sizes, colors and variations, and can be worn by young and old, married and unmarried people alike. Wearing a bindi has become more of a fashion statement than a religious custom.

53. Why did people in India start wearing a red dot on their forehead?
   (A) To indicate their social rank.
   (B) To show their religious belief.
   (C) To display their financial status.
   (D) To highlight their family background.

54. What is the significance of the third eye in Hindu tradition?
   (A) To stay in harmony with nature.
   (B) To observe the outside world more clearly.
   (C) To pay respect to God.
   (D) To see things with a subjective view.

55. Why was red chosen as the original color of the bindi?
   (A) The red dot represented the blood of God.
   (B) Red stood for a wife's love for her husband.
   (C) The word "bindi" means "red" in some Hindi dialects.
   (D) Red was supposed to bring blessings to a married couple.

56. Which of the following statements is true about the practice of wearing a bindi today?
   (A) Bindis are worn anywhere on the face now.
   (B) Bindis are now used as a decorative item.
   (C) Most Indian women do not like to wear bindis anymore.
   (D) Wearing a bindi has become more popular among Indian men.

第貳部份：非選擇題（占 28 分）

一、中譯英（占 8 分）

說明： 1. 請將以下中文句子譯成正確、通順、達意的英文，並將答案寫在「答案卷」上。
　　　 2. 請依序作答，並標明題號。每題 4 分，共 8 分。

　1. 都會地區的高房價對社會產生了嚴重的影響。
　2. 政府正推出新的政策，以滿足人們的住房需求。

二、英文作文（占 20 分）

說明： 1. 依提示在「答案卷」上寫一篇英文作文。
　　　 2. 文長至少 120 個單詞（words）。

提示： 請仔細觀察以下三幅連環圖片的內容，並想像第四幅圖片可能的發展，寫出一個涵蓋連環圖片內容並有完整結局的故事。

102年度學科能力測驗英文科試題詳解

第壹部分：單選題

一、詞彙：

1. (**B**) It rained so hard yesterday that the baseball game had to be <u>postponed</u> until next Saturday.
   昨天雨下得很大，以致於棒球比賽必須<u>延期</u>到下週六。
   (A) surrender〔sə'rɛndə〕v. 投降
   (B) *postpone*〔post'pon〕v. 延期【92 學測也考過】(= *put off*)
   (C) abandon〔ə'bændən〕v. 拋棄
   (D) oppose〔ə'poz〕v. 反對
   hard〔hɑrd〕adv. 猛烈地

2. (**C**) As more people rely on the Internet for information, it has <u>replaced</u> newspapers as the most important source of news.
   隨著有更多人依賴網路取得資訊，網路已經<u>取代</u>報紙，成為最重要的新聞來源。
   (A) distribute〔dɪ'strɪbjut〕v. 分配
   (B) subtract〔səb'trækt〕v. 減去；扣除
   (C) *replace*〔rɪ'ples〕v. 取代【94 學測也考過】
   (D) transfer〔træns'fɝ〕v. 轉移
   rely on 依賴　　*the Internet* 網路
   information〔ˌɪnfə'meʃən〕n. 資訊
   source〔sors〕n. 來源

3. (**A**) Having saved enough money, Joy <u>booked</u> two trips for this summer vacation, one to France and the other to Australia.
   在存夠錢之後，喬伊<u>預訂</u>了兩趟暑假的旅程，一趟去法國，一趟去澳洲。
   (A) *book*〔buk〕v. 預訂　　　　(B) observe〔əb'zɝv〕v. 觀察
   (C) enclose〔ɪn'kloz〕v.（隨函）附寄
   (D) deposit〔dɪ'pazɪt〕v. 存（款）
   Australia〔ɔ'streljə〕n. 澳洲

4. (**D**) Since I do not fully understand your proposal, I am not in the position to make any <u>comment</u> on it.

因為我並沒有完全了解你的提議，我沒有資格做任何<u>評論</u>。

(A) difference〔'dɪfərəns〕*n.* 不同

(B) solution〔sə'luʃən〕*n.* 解決之道

(C) demand〔dɪ'mænd〕*n.* 要求

(D) ***comment***〔'kɑmɛnt〕*n.* 評論　　***make a comment on*** 評論

fully〔'fʊlɪ〕*adv.* 完全地

proposal〔prə'pozḷ〕*n.* 提議　　position〔pə'zɪʃən〕*n.* 立場

in a position to V. 有資格～；能夠～

5. (**C**) Betty was <u>reluctant</u> to accept her friend's suggestion because she thought she could come up with a better idea herself.

貝蒂<u>不願意</u>接受她朋友的建議，因為她覺得她自己可以想出更好的主意。

(A) tolerable〔'tɑlərəbḷ〕*adj.* 可容忍的

(B) sensitive〔'sɛnsətɪv〕*adj.* 敏感的

(C) ***reluctant***〔rɪ'lʌktənt〕*adj.* 勉強的；不願意的

(D) modest〔'mɑdɪst〕*adj.* 謙虛的

come up with 想出

6. (**B**) The bank tries its best to attract more customers. Its staff members are always available to provide <u>prompt</u> service

這家銀行竭盡所能來吸引更多顧客。職員們總是可以提供<u>即時的</u>服務。

(A) singular〔'sɪŋgjələ˞〕*adj.* 單數的

(B) ***prompt***〔prɑmpt〕*adj.* 迅速的；即時的

(C) expensive〔ɪk'spɛnsɪv〕*adj.* 昂貴的

(D) probable〔'prɑbəbḷ〕*adj.* 可能的

try one's best 盡力　　attract〔ə'trækt〕*v.* 吸引|

customer〔'kʌstəmə˞〕*n.* 顧客　　staff〔stæf〕*n.* 職員

member〔'mɛmbə˞〕*n.* 成員

available〔ə'veləbḷ〕*adj.* 可獲得的；有空的

provide〔prə'vaɪd〕*v.* 提供

7. (**A**) John's part-time experience at the cafeteria is good <u>preparation</u> for running his own restaurant.

約翰在自助餐廳的兼差經驗，對經營自己的餐廳是很好的<u>事先準備</u>。

(A) *preparation* (ˌprɛpəˈreʃən) *n.* 準備
(B) recognition (ˌrɛkəgˈnɪʃən) *n.* 認知；認可
(C) formation (fɔrˈmeʃən) *n.* 形成
(D) calculation (ˌkælkjəˈleʃən) *n.* 計算

part-time (ˌpɑrtˈtaɪm) *adj.* 兼差的　　run (rʌn) *v.* 經營

8. (**D**) Women's fashions are <u>constantly</u> changing: One season they may favor pantsuits, but the next season they may prefer miniskirts.

女性時尚<u>不斷</u>在改變：這一季她們可能偏愛褲裝，但是下一季她們可能比較喜歡迷你裙。

(A) lately (ˈletlɪ) *adv.* 最近　　　(B) shortly (ˈʃɔrtlɪ) *adv.* 不久
(C) relatively (ˈrɛlətɪvlɪ) *adv.* 相對地
(D) *constantly* (ˈkɑnstəntlɪ) *adv.* 不斷地

favor (ˈfevɚ) *v.* 偏愛　　　pantsuit (ˈpæntˌsut) *n.* 褲裝
prefer (prɪˈfɝ) *v.* 比較喜歡　　miniskirt (ˈmɪnɪˌskɝt) *n.* 迷你裙

9. (**B**) Standing on the seashore, we saw a <u>flock</u> of seagulls flying over the ocean before they glided down and settled on the water.

站在海邊，我們看到一<u>群</u>海鷗滑翔而下，在水面上棲息，然後飛越海洋。

(A) pack (pæk) *n.* (狗、狼等的) 群
(B) *flock* (flɑk) *n.* (鳥) 群【84 日大也考過】
(C) herd (hɝd) *n.* (牛) 群
(D) school (skul) *n.* (魚) 群

seashore (ˈsiˌʃor) *n.* 海岸　　seagull (ˈsiˌgʌl) *n.* 海鷗
glide (glaɪd) *v.* 滑翔　　settle (ˈsɛtl̩) *v.* 棲息

10. (**C**) The book is not only informative but also <u>entertaining</u>, making me laugh and feel relaxed while reading it.

這本書不僅提供知識，也很<u>有趣</u>，當我閱讀的時候會使我發笑，覺得放鬆。

(A) understanding (ˌʌndɚˈstændɪŋ) *adj.* 體諒的
(B) infect (ɪnˈfɛkt) *v.* 感染
(C) *entertaining* (ˌɛntɚˈtenɪŋ) *adj.* 有趣的

(D) annoying〔ə'nɔɪɪŋ〕*adj.* 煩人的

not only…but also~ 不僅…而且~

informative〔ɪn'fɔrmətɪv〕*adj.* 提供知識的

11. (**C**) After working in front of my computer for the entire day, my neck and shoulders got so <u>stiff</u> that I couldn't even turn my head.
在我的電腦前面工作一整天後，我的脖子和肩膀<u>僵硬</u>到讓我連頭都沒辦法轉。

(A) dense〔dɛns〕*adj.* 密集的；濃密的

(B) harsh〔harʃ〕*adj.* 嚴厲的

(C) ***stiff***〔stɪf〕*adj.* 僵硬的

(D) concrete〔kɑn'krit , 'kɑnkrit〕*adj.* 具體的

in front of 在…前面　　entire〔ɪn'taɪr〕*adj.* 全部的

neck〔nɛk〕*n.* 脖子　　shoulder〔'ʃoldɚ〕*n.* 肩膀

12. (**D**) Getting a flu shot before the start of flu season gives our body a chance to build up protection against the <u>virus</u> that could make us sick. 在流感盛行季節開始前打流感疫苗，能讓我們的身體有機會建立防護，以對抗可能讓我們生病的<u>病毒</u>。

(A) poison〔'pɔɪzn̩〕*n.* 毒藥

(B) misery〔'mɪzərɪ〕*n.* 悲慘

(C) leak〔lik〕*n.* 漏洞　*v.* 漏；漏水

(D) ***virus***〔'vaɪrəs〕*n.* 病毒

flu〔flu〕*n.* 流行性感冒　　shot〔ʃɑt〕*n.* 注射（疫苗）

season〔'sizn̩〕*n.* 季節；時期　　***build up*** 建立

protection〔prə'tɛkʃən〕*n.* 防護

13. (**A**) The kingdom began to <u>collapse</u> after the death of its ruler, and was soon taken over by a neighboring country.
該王國在統治者駕崩後開始<u>瓦解</u>，很快地被鄰國接管。

(A) ***collapse***〔kə'læps〕*v.* 瓦解；倒塌

(B) dismiss〔dɪs'mɪs〕*v.* 下（課）；解僱；解散

(C) rebel〔rɪ'bɛl〕*v.* 反叛

(D) withdraw〔wɪð'drɔ〕*v.* 撤退

kingdom〔'kɪŋdəm〕*n.* 王國

ruler〔'rulɚ〕*n.* 統治者　　***take over*** 接管

neighboring〔'nebərɪŋ〕*adj.* 鄰近的

14. (**D**) Though Kevin failed in last year's singing contest, he did not feel <u>frustrated</u>. This year he practiced day and night and finally won first place in the competition.

雖然凱文去年在歌唱比賽失敗，但是他並沒有感到<u>挫折</u>。今年他日以繼夜地練習，最後在比賽中贏得第一名。

(A) relieved〔rɪˈlivd〕*adj.* 放心的；鬆了一口氣的

(B) suspected〔səˈspɛktɪd〕*adj.* 受到懷疑的

(C) discount〔ˈdɪskaʊnt , dɪsˈkaʊnt〕*v.* 打折

(D) *frustrated*〔ˈfrʌstretɪd〕*adj.* 受挫的

contest〔ˈkɑntɛst〕*n.* 比賽　　***day and night*** 日以繼夜地

first place 第一名　　　competition〔ˌkɑmpəˈtɪʃən〕*n.* 比賽

15. (**C**) Emma and Joe are looking for a live-in babysitter for their three-year-old twins, <u>preferably</u> one who knows how to cook.

艾瑪和喬在為他們的三歲的雙胞胎找一位住在家裡的保姆，<u>最好</u>是會煮飯的人。

(A) initially〔ɪˈnɪʃəlɪ〕*adv.* 起初

(B) apparently〔əˈpærəntlɪ〕*adv.* 明顯地

(C) *preferably*〔ˈprɛfərəblɪ〕*adv.* 最好

(D) considerably〔kənˈsɪdərəblɪ〕*adv.* 相當大地

look for 尋找　　　live-in〔ˈlɪvˈɪn〕*adj.* 住在家裡的；宿於工作處的

babysitter〔ˈbebɪˌsɪtɚ〕*n.* 保姆　　　twins〔twɪnz〕*n. pl.* 雙胞胎

二、綜合測驗：

An area code is a section of a telephone number which generally represents the geographical area that the phone receiving the call is based in. It is the two or three digits just before the local number. If the number <u>being called</u> is in the same area as the number making the call, an area code
16
usually doesn't need to be dialed. The local number, <u>on the other hand</u>,
17
must always be dialed in its entirety.

　　區域號碼是電話號碼的一個部分，通常代表收訊的電話所處的地理位置。它是本地電話號碼之前的二到三碼。若是被撥打的電話與撥打的電話處在相同的區域，撥號時通常不需要輸入區域號碼。然而，本地號碼永遠必須被原封不動地輸入。

area code 區域號碼　　section〔'sɛkʃən〕n. 部分
generally〔'dʒɛnərəlɪ〕adv. 通常　　represent〔ˌrɛprɪ'zɛnt〕v. 代表
geographical〔ˌdʒiə'græfɪkl̩〕adj. 地理的
be based in 以…為基地　　digit〔'dɪdʒɪt〕n.（各個）阿拉伯數字
local〔'lokl̩〕adj. 當地的　　dial〔'daɪəl〕v. 撥（號）
entirety〔ɪn'taɪətɪ〕n. 全體　　**in its entirety** 原封不動；全部

16.（ **B** ）依句意，「被撥打的」電話號碼，須用被動語態，故可用形容詞子句
　　 which is called 修飾先行詞 number，也可省略關代 which，並將 be
　　 動詞 is 改為現在分詞 being，故選 (B) **being called**。【101 指考也考過】

17.（ **D** ）依句意，選 (D) **on the other hand**「另一方面；然而」。【87 學測也考過】
　　 而 (A) in fact「事實上」，(B) to illustrate「為了要說明」，(C) at the
　　 same time「同時」，均不合句意。

　　 The area code was introduced in the United States in 1947. It was
created <u>in</u> the format of XYX, with X being any number between 2-9 and Y
　　　　 18
being either 1 or 0. Cities and areas with higher populations would have a
smaller first and third digit, and 1 as the center digit. New York, being the
largest city in the United States, was <u>assigned</u> the 212 area code, followed
by Los Angeles at 213.　　　　　 19

　　 區域號碼於 1947 年被引進美國。它以 XYX 的形式被創造出來，X 為 2 到
9 之間的任何數字，而 Y 為 1 或是 0。擁有較多人口的城市或區域的第一碼與
第三碼數字會比較小，而中間的第二碼會是 1。美國最大城紐約的區域號碼被
指定為 212，接著是洛杉磯的 213。

　　　　　 introduce〔ˌɪntrə'djus〕v. 引進；採用　　create〔krɪ'et〕v. 創造
　　　　　 format〔'fɔrmæt〕n. 形式；格式
　　　　　 center〔'sɛntɚ〕adj. 中心的；中央的　　**followed by** 接著就是

18.（ **D** ）**in…format** 以…形式

19.（ **B** ）(A) reserve〔rɪ'zɝv〕v. 預訂；保留
　　　　　 (B) **assign**〔ə'saɪn〕v. 分配；分派；指定
　　　　　 (C) represent〔ˌrɛprɪ'zɛnt〕v. 代表
　　　　　 (D) assemble〔ə'sɛmbl̩〕v. 裝配；集合

In countries other than the United States and Canada, the area code
generally determines the <u>cost</u> of a call. Calls within an area code and often
20
a small group of neighboring area codes are normally charged at a lower
rate than outside the area code.

在美國與加拿大之外的國家，區域號碼往往決定了通話的費用。比起處於
區域號碼之外的地區，區域號碼之內或是一小組鄰近區域號碼之間的通話，通
常會被以比較低的費率計費。

> ***other than*** 除了…之外　　determine〔dɪˋtɜmɪn〕*v.* 決定
> neighboring〔ˋnebərɪŋ〕*adj.* 鄰近的；附近的
> normally〔ˋnɔrmḷɪ〕*adv.* 通常　　charge〔tʃɑrdʒ〕*v.* 收費
> rate〔ret〕*n.* 費用；價格
> outside〔autˋsaɪd〕*prep.* 在…的外面

20. (**A**) 依句意，選 (A) ***cost*** 「費用」。而 (B) format 「方式；格式」，(C) quality
「品質」，(D) distance 「距離」，均不合句意。

For coin collectors who invest money in coins, the value of a coin is
determined by various factors. First, scarcity is a major determinant.
<u>The rarer</u> a coin is, the more it is worth. Note, however, that rarity has
21
little to do with the <u>age</u> of a coin. Many thousand-year-old coins often sell
22
for no more than a few dollars because there are a lot of them around, <u>while</u>
23
a 1913 Liberty Head Nickel may sell for over one million US dollars
because there are only five in existence.

對於把錢投資於硬幣的硬幣收藏家來說，有許多決定硬幣價值的要素。首
先，稀有度是一個主要的決定因素。一個硬幣越是稀有，就越是值錢。但是，
請注意，稀有度與硬幣的年份沒什麼關聯。很多千年古幣賣不了多少錢，因為
到處都找得到，然而 1913 年的自由女神頭像五分硬幣售價可能超過一百萬美
金，因為全世界只剩五枚。

> coin〔kɔɪn〕*n.* 硬幣　　collector〔kəˋlɛktə〕*n.* 收集者；收藏者
> invest〔ɪnˋvɛst〕*v.* 投資　　various〔ˋvɛrɪəs〕*adj.* 各種的；各式各樣的
> factor〔ˋfæktə〕*n.* 因素　　scarcity〔ˋskɛrsətɪ〕*n.* 缺乏；不足；稀少

major〔'medʒɚ〕*adj.* 主要的
determinant〔dɪ'tɜmənənt〕*n.* 決定因素
worth〔wɜθ〕*adj.* 有…價值的　　note〔not〕*v.* 注意
rarity〔'rɛrətɪ〕*n.* 稀有；罕見
have little to do with 和…沒什麼關聯
no more than 僅僅；只是（= *only*）
around〔ə'raʊnd〕*adj.* 存在的；在大量出現
liberty〔'lɪbɚtɪ〕*n.* （硬幣上的）自由女神像
nickel〔'nɪkl̩〕*n.* 五分錢硬幣　　***in existence*** 現存的；存在著的

21. (**D**)　「the +比較級…the +比較級」表「越…就越~」，故選 (D) ***The rarer***。
　　　 rare〔rɛr〕*adj.* 稀有的

22. (**A**)　依句意，稀有性和硬幣的「年份」沒什麼關係，故選 (A) ***age*** 「年齡；
　　　 年代」。而 (B) shape「形狀」，(C) size「大小；尺寸」，(D) weight「重
　　　 量」，均不合句意。

23. (**B**)　表示「對比」，連接詞須用 ***while*** 「然而」，選 (B)。【84 學測考過 while
　　　 作「當…的時候」解；93 指考則考 while 作「雖然」解。】而 (A) since「自
　　　 從；既然；因爲」，(C) whether「是否；不論」，(D) if「如果」，均
　　　 不合句意。

Furthermore, the demand for a particular coin will also <u>greatly</u> influence
　　　　　　　　　　　　　　　　　　　　　　　　　　　　24
coin values.　Some coins may command higher prices because they are
more popular with collectors.　For example, a 1798 dime is much rarer than
a 1916 dime, but the <u>latter</u> sells for significantly more, simply because many
　　　　　　　　　　　　25
more people collect early 20th century dimes than dimes from the 1700s.
此外，對某種特定硬幣的需求也將大大影響硬幣的價值。某些硬幣可以賣出比
較高的價錢，因爲它們在收藏家之間較受歡迎。例如，一枚 1798 年的一角硬幣
遠比一枚 1916 年的一角硬幣罕見，但後者的售價卻高得多，僅僅只是因爲收藏
二十世紀早期一角硬幣的人，比收藏十八世紀一角硬幣的人多得多。

furthermore〔'fɜðɚ‚mor〕*adv.* 此外；而且
demand〔dɪ'mænd〕*n.* 需求　　particular〔pɚ'tɪkjələ〕*adj.* 特定的
influence〔'ɪnfluəns〕*v.* 影響

> command〔kə'mænd〕v.（商品）可賣（高價錢）
> dime〔daɪm〕n. 一角硬幣　　rare〔rɛr〕adj. 稀有的
> ***the 1700s*** 十八世紀

24. (**C**) 依句意，對特定硬幣的需求，會「大大地」影響硬幣的價值，故選
　　　 (C) ***greatly***。而 (A) merely「僅僅；只是」, (B) hardly「幾乎不」,
　　　 (D) roughly〔'rʌflɪ〕adv. 粗略地；大約，均不合句意。

25. (**C**) 依句意，選 (C) ***the latter***「後者」。

　　French psychologist Alfred Binet (1859-1911) took a different approach
from most other psychologists of his day:　He was interested in the workings
of the <u>normal</u> mind rather than the nature of mental illness.　He wanted to
　　　　　　26
find a way to measure the ability to think and reason, apart from education
in any particular field.

　　法國心理學家艾爾佛‧比奈（1859-1911）與當時的大部分的心理學家採取
不同門徑：他的興趣在於正常心靈的運作而非精神疾病的性質。在任何特定領
域的教育之外，他想要找到一個方法，去衡量人類思考與推論的能力。

> psychologist〔saɪ'kɑlədʒɪst〕n. 心理學家
> Alfred Binet〔'ælfrɛd bɪ'ne〕n. 艾爾佛‧比內【1857-1911，法國心理學家】
> approach〔ə'protʃ〕n. 方法　　***of one's day*** 某人的那個時代
> ***be interested in*** 對…有興趣
> workings〔'wɜkɪŋz〕n. pl. 工作；運行；活動
> ***rather than*** 而不是　　nature〔'netʃɚ〕n. 特質；特性
> measure〔'mɛʒɚ〕v. 測量；衡量　　reason〔'rizn〕v. 推論
> ***apart from*** 除了…之外　　field〔fild〕n. 領域

26. (**B**) 依句意，選 (B) ***normal***〔'nɔrml〕adj. 正常的；一般的。而 (A) contrary
　　　〔'kɑntrɛrɪ〕adj. 相反的, (C) detective〔dɪ'tɛktɪv〕adj. 偵探的, (D)
　　　mutual〔'mutʃuəl〕adj. 相互的，則不合句意。

　　In 1905 he developed a test in which he <u>had</u> children do tasks such as follow
　　　　　　　　　　　　　　　　　　　　27
commands, copy patterns, name objects, and put things in order or arrange
them properly.　He later created a standard of measuring children's

intelligence <u>based on</u> the data he had collected from the French children he
　　　　　　　28
studied. If 70 percent of 8-year-olds could pass a particular test, then
<u>success</u> on the test represented an 8-year-old's level of intelligence.
　29

1905 年，他發展出一套測試，在這個測試中，他要求孩童完成一些任務，像是依指令行事、依模式模仿、指認物體、將物品依順序擺放或是妥善排列整理等等。之後，依據從受測的法國孩童收集而成的數據，他創造了一套衡量孩童智力的標準。如果百分之七十的八歲小孩能夠通過某項特定測試，則這項測試的成功通過，便可代表八歲孩童的智力水準。

develop〔dɪ'vɛləp〕v. 研發　　task〔tæsk〕n. 任務；工作
follow〔'falo〕v. 遵守　　command〔kə'mænd〕n. 命令；指揮
copy〔'kapɪ〕v. 模仿；複製　　pattern〔'pætən〕n. 模式
name〔nem〕v. 說出…的（正確）名字
object〔'abdʒɪkt〕n. 東西；物體
order〔'ɔrdɚ〕n. 順序；次序　　arrange〔ə'rendʒ〕v. 整理；排列
properly〔'prapəlɪ〕adv. 適當地　　later〔'letɚ〕adv. 後來
standard〔'stændəd〕n. 標準
intelligence〔ɪn'tɛlədʒəns〕n. 智力
data〔'detə〕n. pl. 資料　　study〔'stʌdɪ〕v. 研究
represent〔ˌrɛprɪ'zɛnt〕v. 代表　　level〔'lɛvl̩〕n. 水平；程度

27. (**A**) 由受詞 children 後的原形動詞 do 可知，空格應填使役動詞，故選
(A) *had*。　　*have sb. V.* 叫某人（做）…
而 (B) kept「使…停留在（某種狀態）」，接受詞後須接補語，在此用
法與句意皆不合；(C) wanted「想要」和 (D) asked「要求」，為一般
動詞，接受詞後須接不定詞，用法不合。

28. (**B**) 依句意，選 (B) *based on*「根據」。
而 (A) composed of「由…組成」，(C) resulting in「導致；造成」，
(D) fighting against「與…作戰」，則不合句意。

29. (**A**) 依句意，「成功」通過測驗，選 (A) *success*。
(B) objection〔əb'dʒɛkʃən〕n. 反對
(C) agreement〔ə'grimənt〕n. 同意；協議
(D) discovery〔dɪ'skʌvərɪ〕n. 發現

From Binet's work, the phrase "intelligence quotient" ("IQ") entered the
English vocabulary. The IQ is the ratio of "mental age" to chronological
age times 100, with 100 <u>being</u> the average. So, an 8-year-old who passes
30
the 10-year-old's test would have an IQ of 10/8 times 100, or 125.

因為比奈的研究，智力商數（智商）這個用語進入了英語詞彙。智商，便是「心
理年齡」與實際年齡的比率乘上一百，而一百是平均值。因此，一個能夠通過
十歲測驗的八歲孩童，便擁有十除以八再乘以一百的智商，也就是智商一二五。

> work〔w₃k〕 *n.* 工作成果　　phrase〔frez〕 *n.* 片語；說法
> quotient〔ˈkwoʃənt〕 *n.* 商數
> ***intelligence quotient*** 智力商數；智商（＝*IQ*）
> vocabulary〔vəˈkæbjə͵lɛrɪ〕 *n.* 字彙　　ratio〔ˈreʃo〕 *n.* 比例
> ***mental age*** 智力年齡；心理年齡
> chronological〔͵krɑnəˈlɑdʒɪkḷ〕 *adj.* 按年代順序的
> ***chronological age*** 按時間計算的年齡
> times〔taɪmz〕 *prep.* 乘以　　average〔ˈævərɪdʒ〕 *n.* 平均數；平均值
> or〔ɔr〕 *conj.* 也就是

30. (**D**) with 表附帶狀態，其用法為：「with＋O.＋p.p 或 V-ing」，依句意為主
　　　動，故選 (D) ***being***。【83 夜大也考過】

三、文意選填：

　　Often called "rainforests of the sea," coral reefs provide a home for
25% of all species in the ocean. They are stony structures full of dark
hideaways where fish and sea animals can lay their eggs and [31](**D**) escape
from predators. Without these underwater "apartment houses," there
would be fewer fish in the ocean. Some species might even become
[32](**I**) endangered or disappear completely.

　　常有「海中雨林」美稱的珊瑚礁為整個海洋百分之二十五的物種提供了家
園。它們是充滿黑暗隱蔽處的堅硬結構，魚類及海洋生物可在其中產卵以及躲
避掠食者。要是沒了這些海中的「公寓」，海裡的魚類可能會變少。有些物種甚
至可能會瀕臨絕種或完全消失。

> rainforest〔ˈren͵fɔrɪst〕 *n.* 雨林　　coral〔ˈkɔrəl〕 *n.* 珊瑚
> reef〔rif〕 *n.* 礁　　***coral reef*** 珊瑚礁

species〔'spiʃɪz〕*n.* 物種
stony〔'stonɪ〕*adj.* 石頭的；非常堅硬的
structure〔'strʌktʃɚ〕*n.* 構造
hideaway〔'haɪə,we〕*n.* 躲藏處；藏匿處　　lay〔le〕*v.* 下（蛋）
egg〔ɛg〕*n.* 蛋；卵　　***escape from*** 從…逃脫
predator〔'prɛdətɚ〕*n.* 捕食者
underwater〔'ʌndɚ,wɔtɚ〕*adj.* 水中的
apartment〔ə'pɑrtmənt〕*n.* 公寓
endangered〔ɪn'dendʒɚd〕*adj.* 有危險的；瀕臨絕種的
completely〔kəm'plitlɪ〕*adv.* 完全地

There are thousands of reefs in the world; [33]**(E) sadly**, however, they are now in serious danger. More than one-third are in such bad shape that they could die within ten years. Many might not even [34]**(C) last** that long! Scientists are working hard to find out what leads to this destruction. There are still a lot of questions unanswered, but three main causes have been [35]**(B) identified**.【98學測也考過】

世界上有數千種珊瑚礁；然而，悲傷的是，它們現在的處境極其危險。三分之一以上的狀態已經糟到可能會在十年之內死亡。很多可能甚至沒辦法撐那麼久！科學家努力要尋找造成此種毀滅的原因。目前仍有許多問題未解，但三個主因已被指認出來。

sadly〔'sædlɪ〕*adv.* 可悲的是；遺憾的是　　***in danger*** 有危險
one-third 三分之一　　shape〔ʃep〕*n.* 情形；狀況
find out 查出　　last〔læst〕*v.* 持續；支撐；繼續存在
lead to 導致；造成　　destruction〔dɪ'strʌkʃən〕*n.* 破壞
unanswered〔ʌn'ænsɚd〕*adj.* 無回答的　　main〔men〕*adj.* 主要的
cause〔kɔz〕*n.* 原因　　identify〔aɪ'dɛntə,faɪ〕*v.* 辨識；確認

The first cause is pollution on land. The pollutants run with rainwater into rivers and streams, which [36]**(J) carry** the poisons into the ocean. Chemicals from the poisons kill reefs or make them weak, so they have less [37]**(A) resistance** to diseases.

第一個原因是陸地上的污染。污染物會隨著雨水流入河流與小溪，而溪流會將這些毒物帶入海洋。這些毒物中的化學物質會殺死或弱化珊瑚礁，讓它們對疾病的抵抗力變小。

pollution〔pə'luʃən〕*n.* 污染　　pollutant〔pə'lutənt〕*n.* 污染物
run〔rʌn〕*v.* 流　　rainwater〔'ren,wotə〕*n.* 雨水
stream〔strim〕*n.* 溪流　　carry〔'kærɪ〕*v.* 攜帶
poison〔'pɔɪzn̩〕*n.* 毒；毒藥　　chemical〔'kɛmɪkl̩〕*n.* 化學物質
weak〔wik〕*adj.* 虛弱的　　resistant〔rɪ'zɪstənt〕*adj.* 有抵抗力的
disease〔dɪ'ziz〕*n.* 疾病

Global warming is another reason. Higher ocean temperatures kill the
important food source for the coral—the algae, the tiny greenish-gold water
plants that live on coral. When the algae die, the coral loses its color and
it also dies [38](F) eventually. This process, known as "coral bleaching," has
happened more and more frequently in recent years.

　　另一個原因是全球暖化。較高的海水溫度會殺死珊瑚的重要食物來源——
海藻，也就是那些棲居於珊湖上金金綠綠的微小水生植物。當海藻死去，珊瑚
會失去顏色，然後最終也會死去。近年來，這個被稱爲「珊瑚白化」的過程越
來越常發生。

global warming 全球暖化　　reason〔'rizn̩〕*n.* 理由
temperature〔'tɛmpərətʃə〕*n.* 溫度　　source〔sors〕*n.* 來源
algae〔'ældʒi〕*n. pl.* 海藻　　tiny〔'taɪnɪ〕*adj.* 微小的
greenish〔'grinɪʃ〕*adj.* 帶綠色的
eventually〔ɪ'vɛntʃʊəlɪ〕*adv.* 最後
process〔'prɑsɛs〕*n.* 過程　　*be known as* 被稱爲
bleach〔blitʃ〕*v.* 漂白；變白　　*coral bleaching* 珊瑚白化
more and more 越來越　　recent〔'risn̩t〕*adj.* 最近的

The last factor contributing to the [39](G) disappearance of coral reefs is
people. People sometimes crash into reefs with their boats or drop anchors
on them, breaking off large chunks of coral. Divers who walk on reefs can
also do serious damage. Moreover, some people even break coral off to
collect for [40](H) souvenirs since it is so colorful and pretty.

　　促使珊瑚礁消失的最後一個因素是人類。有時候人類會駛船撞上珊瑚礁，
或是在珊瑚礁上落錨，讓珊瑚礁大塊大塊地剝落。那些在珊瑚礁上步行的潛水
者也會對其造成嚴重損害。此外，因其多彩斑斕而賞心悅目，有些人甚至會扯
落珊瑚礁當作紀念品收藏。

contribute to 促成；造成　　disappearance〔͵dɪsə'pɪrəns〕*n.* 消失
crash into 猛然撞上　　drop〔drɑp〕*v.* 放下
anchor〔'æŋkæ〕*n.* 錨　　**break off** 折斷　　chunk〔tʃʌŋk〕*n.* 厚塊
diver〔'daɪvæ〕*n.* 潛水者　　**do damage** 造成損害
souvenir〔͵suvə'nɪr〕*n.* 紀念品　　colorful〔'kʌləfəl〕*adj.* 五顏六色的

How can we help the reefs? We need to learn more about them and work together to stop the activities that may threaten their existence.

我們要如何幫助珊瑚礁？我們必須對它們有更加充分的認識，並且攜手停止那些可能威脅其生存的活動。

learn〔lɜn〕*v.* 知道　　**work together** 合作
activity〔æk'tɪvətɪ〕*n.* 活動　　threaten〔'θrɛtn̩〕*v.* 威脅
existance〔ɪg'zɪstəns〕*n.* 存在

四、閱讀測驗：

41-44 為題組

The Swiss army knife is a popular device that is recognized all over the world. In Switzerland, there is a saying that every good Swiss citizen has one in his or her pocket. But the knife had humble beginnings.

瑞士軍刀是個受歡迎的工具，受到全世界的認可。在瑞士，有一句話說，每位瑞士的公民的口袋裡都有一把瑞士刀。但是這刀子出身卑微。

Swiss〔swɪs〕*adj.* 瑞士的　　army〔'ɑrmɪ〕*adv.* 軍隊的　　*n.* 軍隊
knife〔naɪf〕*n.* 小刀　　**Swiss army knife** 瑞士軍刀
device〔dɪ'vaɪs〕*n.* 器具
recognize〔'rɛkəg͵naɪz〕*v.* 認可　　**all over the world** 全世界
Switzerland〔'swɪtsəlænd〕*n.* 瑞士【歐洲中部的一聯邦共和國】
saying〔'se·ɪŋ〕*n.* 諺語；俗話　　citizen〔'sɪtəzn̩〕*n.* 市民；公民
pocket〔'pɑkɪt〕*n.* 口袋　　humble〔'hʌmbl̩〕*adj.* 卑微的
beginning〔bɪ'gɪnɪŋ〕*n.* 起源

In the late nineteenth century, the Swiss army issued its soldiers a gun that required a special screwdriver to dismantle and clean it. At the same time, canned food was becoming common in the army. Swiss generals decided to issue each soldier a standard knife to serve both as a screwdriver and a can opener.

在十九世紀晚期，瑞士軍隊發給每位士兵一支槍，這槍需要用專用的螺絲起子才能拆解並清理。同時，罐頭食品在軍隊裡變得普遍。瑞士的將軍們決定發給每位士兵一把標準規格的刀子，用來當作螺絲起子和開罐器。

century〔ˋsɛntʃərɪ〕n. 世紀　　issue〔ˋɪʃʊ〕v. 發送；配給
soldier〔ˋsoldʒɚ〕n. 軍人；士兵　　gun〔gʌn〕n. 槍
require〔rɪˋkwaɪr〕v. 需要　　special〔ˋspɛʃəl〕adj. 特殊的；專用的
screwdriver〔ˋskru͵draɪvɚ〕n. 螺絲起子
dismantle〔dɪsˋmæntḷ〕v. 拆解　　clean〔klin〕v. 清理
at the same time 同時　　canned〔kænd〕adj. 罐裝的
canned food 罐頭食品　　common〔ˋkɑmən〕adj. 普遍的
general〔ˋdʒɛnərəl〕n. 將軍　　standard〔ˋstændɚd〕adj. 標準的
serve as 充當　　*can opener* 開罐器

It was a lifesaver for Swiss knife makers, who were struggling to compete with cheaper German imports. In 1884, Carl Elsener, head of the Swiss knife manufacturer Victorinox, seized that opportunity with both hands, and designed a soldier's knife that the army loved. It was a simple knife with one big blade, a can opener, and a screwdriver.

對於正奮力與德國廉價進口刀競爭的瑞士製刀商來說，這消息如同救星。在1884年，瑞士刀製造商維氏的總裁，卡爾·埃森納，抓緊了這個機會，並設計了受軍隊所愛的士兵用刀。這把小刀的構造很簡單，有一把大的刀身、一個開罐器和一個螺絲起子。

lifesaver〔ˋlaɪf͵sevɚ〕n. 救星　　maker〔ˋmekɚ〕n. 製造者
struggle〔ˋstrʌgḷ〕v. 掙扎；努力要
compete〔kəmˋpit〕v. 競爭　　German〔ˋdʒɝmən〕adj. 德國的
import〔ˋɪmport〕n. 進口品
Carl Elsener 卡爾·埃森納【瑞士刀創始者】
head〔hɛd〕n. 總裁
manufacturer〔͵mænjəˋfæktʃərɚ〕n. 製造業者；製造公司
Victorinox 維氏【瑞士軍刀製造商，卡爾·埃森納以母親的名字維多利亞(Victoria)命名】
seize〔siz〕v. 抓住　　opportunity〔͵ɑpɚˋtjunətɪ〕n. 機會
with both hands 全力地　　design〔dɪˋzaɪn〕v. n. 設計
blade〔bled〕n. 刀片；刀身

A few years after the soldier's knife was issued, the "Schweizer Offizier Messer," or Swiss Officer's Knife, came on the market.

Interestingly, the Officer's Knife was never given to those serving in the army. The Swiss military purchasers considered the new model with a corkscrew for opening wine not "essential for survival," so officers had to buy this new model by themselves. But its special multi-functional design later launched the knife as a global brand. After the Second World War, a great number of American soldiers were stationed in Europe. And as they could buy the Swiss army knife at shops on military bases, they bought huge quantities of them. However, it seems that "Schweizer Offizier Messer" was too difficult for them to say, so they just called it the Swiss army knife, and that is the name it is now known by all over the world.

　　在發給士兵小刀幾年後，"Schweizer Offizier Messer"，也就是「瑞士軍官刀」，就上市了。有趣的是，軍官刀從來沒發給那些從軍的人。瑞士軍方的採買者認爲這種附有開酒拔塞鑽的新刀款「對生存而言並非必要」，所以軍官想要這種新刀款的話，必須自掏腰包購買。但是這款獨有的多功能設計後來讓這款刀發售後，成爲全球性的品牌。二次大戰後，很多美國士兵派駐在歐洲。而因爲他們能夠在軍事基地的商店買到瑞士刀，他們便大量購買。然而，"Schweizer Offizier Messer"對他們來說似乎太難念了，所以他們就稱它爲瑞士軍刀，這個名字也就聞名於全世界。

officer〔ˋɔfəsɚ〕 *n.* 軍官　　***on the market*** 出售；上市
interestingly〔ˋɪntrəstɪŋlɪ〕 *adv.* 有趣地；有趣的是
serve〔sɝv〕 *v.* 任職；服役　　***serve in the army*** 從軍
military〔ˋmɪləˌtɛrɪ〕 *adj.* 軍事的　　purchaser〔ˋpɝtʃəsɚ〕 *n.* 購買者
consider〔kənˋsɪdɚ〕 *v.* 認爲　　model〔ˋmɑdl̩〕 *n.* 模型；款式
corkscrew〔ˋkɔrkˌskru〕 *n.* 拔塞鑽；螺絲錐
essential〔əˋsɛnʃəl〕 *adj.* 必要的；不可或缺的
survival〔səˋvaɪvl̩〕 *n.* 生存　　multi-〔ˋmʌltɪ〕 多⋯
functional〔ˋfʌŋkʃənl̩〕 *adj.* 功能的　　launch〔lɔntʃ〕 *n.* 發行；發售
global〔ˋglobl̩〕 *adj.* 全球的　　brand〔brænd〕 *n.* 品牌
the Second World War 第二次世界大戰
a great number of 很多（= *many*）　　station〔ˋsteʃən〕 *v.* 派駐
base〔bes〕 *n.* 基地　　huge〔hjudʒ〕 *adj.* 龐大的
quantity〔ˋkwɑntətɪ〕 *n.* 數量　　***too ~ to*** ⋯ 太 ~ 以致於不⋯
be known by 以⋯而知名

41. (**A**) 本文的主旨為何？

    (A) 解釋瑞士軍刀的起源。

    (B) 介紹瑞士軍刀的功能。

    (C) 強調瑞士軍刀的重要性。

    (D) 講述一個關於瑞士軍刀設計者的故事。

    explain〔ɪkˋsplen〕v. 解釋　　origin〔ˋɔrədʒɪn〕n. 起源
    introduce〔͵ɪntrəˋdjus〕v. 介紹
    emphasize〔ˋɛmfə͵saɪz〕v. 強調

42. (**A**) 第三段的 "It" 所指的是什麼？

    (A) 瑞士的軍隊需要給每位士兵一把小刀。

    (B) 每位瑞士公民口袋裡都有一把小刀。

    (C) 瑞士刀和進口刀競爭。

    (D) 罐頭食品在瑞士軍隊變得受歡迎。

    imported〔ɪmˋportɪd〕adj. 進口的

43. (**D**) 為什麼瑞士軍方沒有購買瑞士軍官刀？

    (A) 刀的設計太簡單。

    (B) 刀子全賣給了美國士兵

    (C) 軍方沒有預算購買。

    (D) 新的設計對軍官來說被認為沒有擁有的必要。

    sell out 售完　　budget〔ˋbʌdʒɪt〕n. 預算
    purchase〔ˋpɜtʃəs〕n. 購買　　*make a purchase* 購買

44. (**C**) 誰讓文中所討論的刀得到「瑞士軍刀」這個名字？

    (A) 卡爾・埃森納。　　　　(B) 瑞士的軍官。

    (C) 美國士兵。　　　　　　(D) 德國商人。

45-48 為題組

    Space is where our future is—trips to the Moon, Mars and beyond. Most people would think that aside from comets and stars there is little else out there. But, since our space journey started we have left so much trash there that scientists are now concerned that if we don't clean it up, we may all be in mortal danger.

　　我們的未來在太空——探索月球、火星和更遠地方的旅行。大多數的人會認爲除了彗星和星星，沒有什麼其他的東西在太空中。可是，自從我們開始了太空之旅，我們已經在太空留下如此多的垃圾，而現在科學家擔心，如果我們不把它清理乾淨，我們可能全都有生命危險。

space〔spes〕 *n.* 太空　　Moon〔mun〕 *n.* 月球
Mars〔mɑrz〕 *n.* 火星
beyond〔bɪ'jɑnd〕 *adv.* 在更遠處；往更遠處
aside from 除了…之外　　comet〔'kɑmɪt〕 *n.* 彗星
concern〔kən'sɜn〕 *v.* 擔心　　mortal〔'mɔrtl̩〕 *adj.* 致命的

The first piece of space junk was created in 1964, when the American satellite Vanguard I stopped operating and lost its connection with the ground center. However, since it kept orbiting around the Earth without any consequences, scientists became increasingly comfortable abandoning things that no longer served any useful purpose in space.

　　第一個太空垃圾在西元 1964 年被創造出來，那時候是美國的先鋒 1 號衛星停止運轉而且失去與地面中心的連線。然而，因爲它就這樣一直繞著地球運行而沒有造成任何不良後果，科學家們對於把失去用途的東西丟棄在太空中，也越來越不擔心了。

junk〔dʒʌŋk〕 *n.* 垃圾　　satellite〔'sætl̩,aɪt〕 *n.* 衛星
vanguard〔'væn,gɑrd〕 *n.* 先鋒　　operate〔'ɑpə,ret〕 *v.* 運轉
connection〔kə'nɛkʃən〕 *n.* 連線
orbit〔'ɔrbɪt〕 *v.* 繞…的軌道運行
consequence〔'kɑnsə,kwɛns〕 *n.* 結果
increasingly〔ɪn'krisɪŋlɪ〕 *adv.* 越來越
comfortable〔'kʌmfətəbl̩〕 *adj.* 舒服的；自在的
abandon〔ə'bændən〕 *v.* 拋棄　　***no longer*** 不再
serve〔sɜv〕 *v.* 適合　　purpose〔'pɜpəs〕 *n.* 用途

It is estimated that there are currently over 500,000 pieces of man-made trash orbiting the Earth at speeds of up to 17,500 miles per hour. The junk varies from tiny pieces of paint chipped off rockets to cameras, huge fuel tanks, and even odd items like the million-dollar tool kit that astronaut Heidemarie Stefanyshyn-Piper lost during a spacewalk.

目前估計有超過 50 萬件人造垃圾,以最高到每小時 1 萬 7 千 5 百英哩的速度,繞著地球的軌道運行。這些垃圾各異其趣,從火箭上剝落的小漆片,到相機、大型燃料箱,甚至有奇特的物品,像是太空人海德瑪莉・史蒂芬妮欣一派柏在太空漫步時遺失的百萬元工具組。

> estimate〔ˈɛstəˌmet〕v. 估計
> currently〔ˈkɝəntlɪ〕adv. 目前;現在
> man-made〔ˈmænˌmed〕adj. 人造的　　vary〔ˈvɛrɪ〕v. 不同
> tiny〔ˈtaɪnɪ〕adj. 很小的　　　paint〔pent〕n. 油漆
> chip〔tʃɪp〕v. 削去 < off >　　fuel〔ˈfjuəl〕n. 燃料
> tank〔tæŋk〕n.(水、油、氣體等)箱
> odd〔ɑd〕adj. 奇特的　　kit〔kɪt〕n. 一組工具
> astronaut〔ˈæstrəˌnɔt〕n. 太空人
> spacewalk〔ˈspesˌwɔk〕n. 太空漫步

The major problem with the space trash is that it may hit working satellites and damage traveling spacecraft. Moreover, pieces of junk may collide with each other and break into fragments which fall back to the Earth. To avoid this, scientists have devised several ways for clearing the sky. Ground stations have been built to monitor larger pieces of space trash to prevent them from crashing into working satellites or space shuttles. Future plans include a cooperative effort among many nations to stop littering in space and to clean up the trash already there.

太空垃圾的主要問題是,它可能會擊中運作中的衛星和損害旅途中的太空船。此外,垃圾可能會相撞並破成碎片,落回地球。為了避免這樣的情況,科學家們已經想出幾個方法來清掃天空。建造地面站來監測大型太空垃圾,來阻止它們衝撞正在運作的衛星或太空梭。未來的計畫,包括許多國家在內的合作成果,要停止在太空亂丟東西,並將已經在那裡的垃圾清除乾淨。

> major〔ˈmedʒɚ〕adj. 主要的　　work〔wɝk〕v. 運作
> damage〔ˈdæmɪdʒ〕v. 損害　　spacecraft〔ˈspesˌkræft〕n. 太空船
> moreover〔morˈovɚ〕adv. 此外
> collide〔kəˈlaɪd〕v. 相撞 < with >　　devise〔dɪˈvaɪz〕v. 想出
> clear〔klɪr〕v. 從…除去~(障礙物);把…打掃乾淨
> monitor〔ˈmɑnətɚ〕v. 監測　　prevent〔prɪˈvɛnt〕v. 阻止
> space-shuttle〔ˈspesˈʃʌtl̩〕n. 太空梭　　include〔ɪnˈklud〕v. 包括

cooperative〔koˊɑpəˌretɪv〕*adj.* 合作的
effort〔ˊɛfət〕*n.* 努力的成果
among〔əˊmʌŋ〕*prep.* 在…之中　　　litter〔ˊlɪtə〕*v.* 亂丟（東西）

45.（**D**）第一個人造太空垃圾是什麼？
　　(A) 一台相機。　　　　　　　(B) 一組工具。
　　(C) 一個燃料槽。　　　　　　(D) 一架壞掉的衛星。
　　broken〔ˊbrokən〕*adj.* 損壞的

46.（**C**）為什麼一開始科學家們「不」擔心太空垃圾？
　　(A) 它不再適合任何用途。　　(B) 它離地球有幾百萬英里遠。
　　(C) 它沒有造成任何問題。　　(D) 它被認為像彗星和星星。
　　cause〔kɔz〕*v.* 造成　　　regard〔rɪˊgɑrd〕*v.* 認為
　　similar〔ˊsɪmələ〕*adj.* 類似的

47.（**D**）以下關於太空垃圾的敘述，哪一個是真的？
　　(A) 它是大又重的機器。　　　(B) 它從未改變位置。
　　(C) 它繞著地球緩慢飄浮。
　　(D) 它可能對太空梭造成問題。
　　position〔pəˊzɪʃən〕*n.* 位置　　float〔flot〕*v.* 飄浮

48.（**B**）關於太空垃圾的問題，我們已經做了什麼？
　　(A) 科學家們已清除大部份的垃圾。
　　(B) 嚴密監看大型太空垃圾。
　　(C) 很多國家一起合作來停止污染太空。
　　(D) 建造地面站來協助適當地儲存太空垃圾。
　　closely〔ˊkloslɪ〕*adv.* 嚴密地　　watch〔wɑtʃ〕*v.* 監視
　　pollute〔pəˊlut〕*v.* 污染　　store〔stor〕*v.* 儲存
　　properly〔ˊprɑpəlɪ〕*adv.* 適當地

49-52 為題組

　　An alcohol breath test (ABT) is often used by the police to find out whether a person is drunk while driving. In the United States, the legal blood alcohol limit is 0.08% for people aged 21 years or older, while people under 21 are not allowed to drive a car with any level of alcohol in their body. A "positive" test result, a result over the legal limit, allows the police to arrest the driver. However, many people who tested positive on the test have claimed that they only drank a "non-alcoholic" energy drink. Can one of these energy drinks really cause someone to test positive on an ABT? Researchers in Missouri set up an experiment to find out.

酒精呼氣測試常用於警察在查明一個人是否酒後駕車。在美國，21歲以上的人合法的血液酒精濃度限制爲0.08%，而21歲以下的人不允許開車時體內有任何酒精。陽性的酒測結果，也就是超過合法範圍的結果，可以讓警察逮捕駕駛。然而，許多在測試中被測出陽性的人都聲稱他們只喝了「非酒精的」提神飲料。眞的有某種提神飲料會導致某人在酒測時呈陽性反應嗎？密蘇里州的研究員精心設計了一項測試來查明。

alcohol〔'ælkə,hɔl〕*n.* 酒精　　breath〔brɛθ〕*n.* 呼氣
alcohol breath test* (*ABT*)** 酒精呼氣測試　　***find out 查明
drunk〔drʌŋk〕*adj.* 喝醉了的　　legal〔'ligl〕*adj.* 合法的
blood〔blʌd〕*n.* 血液　　limit〔'lɪmɪt〕*n.* 限制
result〔rɪ'zʌlt〕*n.* 結果　　allow〔ə'laʊ〕*v.* 允許
arrest〔ə'rɛst〕*v.* 逮捕　　test〔tɛst〕*v.* 檢驗
positive〔'pɑzətɪv〕*adj.* 陽性的　　claim〔klem〕*v.* 聲稱
non-alcoholic〔nʌn,ælkə'hɔlɪk〕*adj.* 非酒精的
energy〔'ɛnə‑dʒɪ〕*n.* 精力　　drink〔drɪŋk〕*n.* 飲料
energy drink 提神飲料　　cause〔kɔz〕*v.* 導致
Missouri〔mə'zʊrɪ〕*n.* 密蘇里州【美國中部之一州】
set up 精心策劃　　experiment〔ɪk'spɛrəmənt〕*n.* 實驗

First, the amount of alcohol in 27 different popular energy drinks was measured. All but one had an alcohol level greater than 0.005%. In nine of the 27 drinks, the alcohol level was at least 0.096%. The scientists then investigated the possibility that these small levels of alcohol could be detected by an ABT. They asked test subjects to drink a full can or bottle of an energy drink and then gave each subject an ABT one minute and 15 minutes after the drink was finished.

　　首先，測量總數為 27 種的提神飲料的酒精濃度。只有一種沒有超過 0.005% 的酒精濃度。27 種裡的 9 種飲料的酒精濃度至少有 0.096%。接下來科學家調查了這些微量的酒精可以被酒測測出來的可能性。他們請被實驗者喝下一整罐或一整瓶的提神飲料，然後在他們喝完後一分鐘及15分鐘時為每個受測者進行酒測。

amount〔ə'maʊnt〕*n.* 總數　　　measure〔'mɛʒɚ〕*v.* 測量
all but 幾乎　　　great〔gret〕*adj.* 多的；大的
investigate〔ɪn'vɛstə,get〕*v.* 調查
possibility〔,pɑsə'bɪlətɪ〕*n.* 可能性　　　detect〔dɪ'tɛkt〕*v.* 查出
subject〔'sʌbdʒɪkt〕*n.* 被實驗者　　　can〔kæn〕*n.* 罐
bottle〔'bɑtl̩〕*n.* 瓶

For 11 of the 27 energy drinks, the ABT did detect the presence of alcohol if the test was given within one minute after the drink was taken. However, alcohol could not be detected for any of the drinks if the test was given 15 minutes after the drink was consumed. This shows that when the test is taken plays a crucial role in the test result. The sooner the test is conducted after the consumption of these drinks, the more likely a positive alcohol reading will be obtained.

　　27 種裡的 11 種提神飲料中，如果在喝完飲料的一分鐘測試的話，酒測確實查出酒精的存在。然而，如果在飲料喝完的 15 分鐘時測試的話，沒有任何飲料的酒精濃度會被測出。這顯示進行測試的時間點，在測試結果中扮演了很重要的角色。在喝完這些飲料後越早執行測試，就越有可能得到陽性的度數。

presence〔'prɛzn̩s〕*n.* 存在
consume〔kən'sjum〕*v.* 消耗；吃；喝
crucial〔'kruʃəl〕*adj.* 非常重要的
play a crucial role 扮演很重要的角色
conduct〔kən'dʌkt〕*v.* 執行
consumption〔kən'sʌmpʃən〕*n.* 消耗
likely〔'laɪklɪ〕*adj.* 有可能的
reading〔'ridɪŋ〕*n.* 指示之度數
obtain〔əb'ten〕*v.* 獲得

49. (**A**) 對一個剛 20 歲的人來說，在美國開車時允許的酒精濃度是多少？
　　(A) <u>0.000%。</u>　　　　　　　(B) 0.005%。
　　(C) 0.080%。　　　　　　　(D) 0.096%。

　　turn〔tɝn〕v. 轉變；成為

50. (**B**) 密蘇里州的實驗目的是什麼？
　　(A) 介紹一種新的計算血液酒精濃度的方法。
　　(B) <u>發掘提神飲料和酒測結果之間的關係。</u>
　　(C) 對喝提神飲料加酒的危險性做出警告。
　　(D) 挑戰美國目前對駕駛的酒精濃度法規。

　　method〔'mɛθəd〕n. 方法
　　calculate〔'kælkjə,let〕v. 計算　　discover〔dɪ'skʌvɚ〕v. 發現
　　relation〔rɪ'leʃən〕n. 關係　　mix〔mɪks〕v. 混合
　　challenge〔'tʃælɪndʒ〕v. 挑戰

51. (**C**) 受實驗者在喝完飲料時被要求做什麼？
　　(A) 在實驗室中排成一列。
　　(B) 回想飲料的品牌。
　　(C) <u>接受酒精呼氣測試。</u>
　　(D) 測試他們呼氣的清新度。

　　participant〔pɚ'tɪsəpənt〕n. 參與者　　***line up*** 排成一列
　　laboratory〔'læbrə,torɪ〕n. 實驗室　　recall〔rɪ'kɔl〕v. 回想
　　brand〔brænd〕n. 品牌　　freshness〔'frɛʃnɪs〕n. 新鮮

52. (**D**) 對提神飲料的消費者而言在接受酒測時什麼是最重要的因素？
　　(A) 受測者的年紀。　　　　　　(B) 進行測試的地方。
　　(C) 測試所用的儀器。　　　　　(D) <u>執行測試的時間點。</u>

　　affect〔ə'fɛkt〕v. 影響　　consumer〔kən'sjumɚ〕n. 消費者
　　equipment〔ɪ'kwɪpmənt〕n. 設備；儀器

53-56 為題組

　　The majority of Indian women wear a red dot between their eyebrows. While it is generally taken as an indicator of their marital status, the practice is primarily related to the Hindu religion.　The dot goes by different names in different Hindi dialects, and "bindi" is the one that is most commonly known. Traditionally, the dot carries no gender restriction: Men as well as women wear it. However, the tradition of men wearing it has faded in recent times, so nowadays we see a lot more women than men wearing one.

　　大多數的印度女性在她們的眉間會點上一個紅點。雖然一般會被視為是顯現她們的婚姻狀態，但這主要還是和印度的習俗有關。這個紅點在印度的方言中有很多不同的名稱，而 bindi 是最常見的說法。傳統上，這個點並不帶有性別的限制，男性女性都可以點。但是，近來男性已經漸漸不會去點它了，所以現在我們會看到眉間點紅點的女性遠多於男性。

majority〔mə'dʒɔrətɪ〕*n.* 大部分；大多數
dot〔dɑt〕*n.* 小點　　　eyebrow〔'aɪ,braʊ〕*n.* 眉毛
be taken as 被視為　　　indicator〔'ɪndə,ketɚ〕*n.* 指標
marital〔'mærətḷ〕*adj.* 婚姻的　　　status〔'stetəs〕*n.* 狀態
practice〔'præktɪs〕*n.* 習俗　　　primarily〔'praɪ,mɛrɪlɪ〕*adv.* 主要地
Hindu〔'hɪndu〕*n.* 印度　　　religion〔rɪ'lɪdʒən〕*n.* 宗教
go〔go〕*v.* 稱為；叫作　　　Hindi〔'hɪndi〕*adj.* 印度語的
dialect〔'daɪə,lɛkt〕*n.* 方言
bindi〔'bɪndi〕*n.*（印度婦女等的）眉心紅點；眉心飾記
carry〔'kærɪ〕*v.* 具有　　　gender〔'dʒɛndɚ〕*n.* 性別
restriction〔rɪ'strɪkʃən〕*n.* 限制　　　**as well as** 以及
fade〔fed〕*v.* 凋謝；枯萎

　　The position of the bindi is standard: center of the forehead, close to the eyebrows. It represents a third, or inner eye. Hindu tradition holds that all people have three eyes: The two outer ones are used for seeing the outside world, and the third one is there to focus inward toward God. As such, the dot signifies piety and serves as a constant reminder to keep God in the front of a believer's thoughts.

　　眉心紅點有標準的位置：接近眉毛的前額中心點。它代表第三隻眼，或者說，內心之眼。印度的傳統習俗認為所有的人都有三隻眼睛：兩隻外面的眼睛看外面的世界，第三隻眼睛向內觀照看神明。紅點本身代表虔誠，也一直提醒信徒們要把神明擺在第一位。

standard〔'stændəd〕*adj.* 標準的　　forehead〔'fɔr,hɛd〕*n.* 前額
represent〔,rɛprɪ'zɛnt〕*v.* 代表　　inner〔'ɪnɚ〕*adj.* 內部的
hold〔hold〕*v.* 認為　　inward〔'ɪnwəd〕*adv.* 向內
as such 就其本身而言　　signify〔'sɪgnə,faɪ〕*v.* 表示
piety〔'paɪətɪ〕*n.* 孝順；虔誠
serve as 充當　　constant〔'kɑnstənt〕*adj.* 持續的
reminder〔rɪ'maɪdɚ〕*n.* 提醒的人或物

Red is the traditional color of the dot. It is said that in ancient times a man would place a drop of blood between his wife's eyes to seal their marriage. According to Hindu beliefs, the color red is believed to bring good fortune to the married couple. Today, people go with different colors depending upon their preferences. Women often wear dots that match the color of their clothes. Decorative or sticker bindis come in all sizes, colors and variations, and can be worn by young and old, married and unmarried people alike. Wearing a bindi has become more of a fashion statement than a religious custom.

眉心上的點傳統顏色是紅色。據說在古代的時候，男性會滴一滴血在妻子的兩眼間，藉以鞏固他們的婚姻。根據印度信仰，紅色可以為夫妻帶來好運。現今，眉心上的點的顏色則是根據個人的喜好而定。女性會搭配衣服選顏色。裝飾或貼上去的點有各種大小尺寸，顏色和樣式，不管年紀大小，已婚或未婚都可以點上。眉心上的點已經比較像是時尚的展現，而不是代表宗教的習俗了。

drop〔drɑp〕*n.* 一滴　　seal〔sil〕*v.* 使堅固
fortune〔'fɔrtʃən〕*n.* 運氣　　***go with*** 適合；相配
depend upon 視…而定；取決於　　preference〔'prɛfrəns〕*n.* 偏好
decorative〔'dɛkə,retɪv〕*adj.* 裝飾的　　sticker〔'stɪkɚ〕*n.* 貼紙
variation〔,vɛrɪ'eʃən〕*n.* 變化
statement〔'stetmənt〕*n.* 陳述；聲明　　custom〔'kʌstəm〕*n.* 習俗

53. (**B**) 為何印度人開始在前額上點上紅點？
　　(A) 表示他們的社會階級。　　(B) <u>表示他們的宗教信仰。</u>
　　(C) 表示他們的財務狀況。　　(D) 強調他們的家庭背景。
indicate〔'ɪndə,ket〕*v.* 表示
belief〔bɪ'lif〕*n.* 信仰　　display〔dɪ'sple〕*v.* 展示
financial〔faɪ'nænʃəl〕*adj.* 財務的　　highlight〔'haɪ,laɪt〕*v.* 強調

54. (**C**) 在印度的傳統中第三隻眼的重要性為何？
(A) 和大自然保持和諧。　　　(B) 能把外面的世界看得更清楚。
(C) 尊敬神明。　　　　　　　(D) 主觀看待事物。

harmony〔'hɑrmənɪ〕*n.* 調和；和諧　　***in harmony with*** 和…調和
subjective〔səb'dʒɛktɪv〕*adj.* 主觀的

55. (**D**) 為什麼人工痣本來是紅色？
(A) 紅點代表神明的血液。
(B) 紅色代表妻子對丈夫的愛。
(C) 在一些印度的方言中，bindi 這個字是紅色的意思。
(D) 紅色會對結婚的夫婦帶來好運。

stand for 代表　　　　blessing〔'blɛsɪŋ〕*n.* 幸福；神恩

56. (**B**) 以下對於現在點上眉心紅點的敘述何者正確？
(A) 眉心紅點可以點在臉上任何一個位置。
(B) 眉心紅點現在變成一種裝飾品。
(C) 大多數的印度女性已經不喜歡點眉心紅點了。
(D) 在印度的男性中，點眉心紅點已經越來越受到歡迎。

第貳部分：非選擇題

一、中譯英

1. 都會地區的高房價對社會產生嚴重的影響。

<u>The high prices of houses / High housing prices</u> in <u>urban / metropolitan</u> areas have a serious <u>effect / influence</u> on society.

2. 政府正推出新的政策，以滿足人們的住房需求。

The government is <u>putting forth / proposing / launching</u> new policies to
<u>meet / satisfy</u> ⎰ people's housing <u>demands / needs.</u>
　　　　　　　⎱ people's <u>demands / needs</u> for housing.

二、英文作文：

　　In the past, George would sit in the Priority Seat while riding the MRT. Sitting there, he would bury his nose in his smartphone, unaware that he was depriving others more deserving of the seat. ***For instance,*** an elderly man once had to stand for 15 minutes because George didn't care enough to give up his seat.

Then one day, George broke his ankle while playing basketball. His foot was in a cast and he had to walk with a crutch. **The very next day**, George was on the MRT and couldn't find a seat. He noticed a young girl about his age sitting in a Priority Seat. He wondered, "Doesn't she see me standing here with a crutch?" Apparently, she did not. George was just about to say something when the elderly man sitting next to the girl spoke up.

"Excuse me, dear," the man said kindly to the girl, "but would you mind giving up your seat for that boy with the crutch?" The girl quickly stood up, offering her seat to George. As he sat down, George realized the importance of Priority Seats and learned a valuable lesson about consideration for others.

priority〔praɪˈɔrətɪ〕*n.* 優先權　　***priority seat*** 博愛座
the MRT 捷運（= *the Mass Rapid Transit*）
bury〔ˈbɛrɪ〕*v.* 埋　　***bury** one's **nose in*** 埋首於；沈迷於
smartphone〔ˈsmɑrtˌfon〕*n.* 智慧型手機
unaware〔ˌʌnəˈwɛr〕*adj.* 不知道的；未察覺的
deprive〔dɪˈpraɪv〕*v.* 剝奪
deserving〔dɪˈzɝvɪŋ〕*adj.* 應得的 < *of* >
for instance 舉例來說　　elderly〔ˈɛldəlɪ〕*adj.* 年長的
give up** one's **seat 讓座　　ankle〔ˈæŋkl̩〕*n.* 腳踝
break** one's **ankle 跌斷腳踝　　cast〔kæst〕*n.* 石膏
in a cast 包石膏　　crutch〔krʌtʃ〕*n.* 拐杖
the next day（過去）隔天　　wonder〔ˈwʌndə〕*v.* 猜想
apparently〔əˈpærəntlɪ〕*adv.* 顯然
be (just) about to V. 即將～；正要～　　***speak up*** 大聲說
mind + V-ing 介意～　　offer〔ˈɔfə〕*v.* 提供
realize〔ˈriəˌlaɪz〕*v.* 了解；領悟
valuable〔ˈvæljəbl̩〕*adj.* 有價值的；珍貴的
learn a lesson 學到教訓
consideration〔kənˌsɪdəˈreʃən〕*n.* 體諒

102 年學測英文科試題修正意見

※ 今年試題製作嚴謹，只有兩個地方需要修正。

題　　號	修　　　正　　　意　　　見
一、詞彙題 第 4 題	I'm not in *the* position to make any comment on it. → I'm not in *a* position to make any comment on it. * 根據句意，應用不定冠詞 a。
四、閱讀測驗 第 50 題	What *is* the purpose of the Missouri experiment? → What *was* the purpose of the Missouri experiment? * 因為實驗已經做過，所以應用過去式。

※ 要特別注意，有人會認為綜合測驗第 20 題答案 (D) distance 也可以，但是如果看到
下一句，其中有 are normally charged at a lower rate（價格），就知道應選 (A) cost。

102 年學測英文科試題出題來源

題　　號	出　　　　　　　　處
一、詞彙 第 1～15 題	所有各題對錯答案的選項，均出自大考中心編製的「學科能力英文常 考字彙表」，像較難的單字 reluctant（不情願的）、stiff（僵硬的）、 prompt（迅速的），都在其中。
二、綜合測驗 第 16～20 題	改寫自 Telephone Numbering Plan（電話數字計畫），敘述區域號碼 產生的歷史。
第 21～25 題	改寫自 Determine the Value of a Coin（決定硬幣的價值），說明各種 決定硬幣價值的方式。
第 26～30 題	改寫自 PEOPLE AND DISCOVERIES（人物與發現），敘述心理學家 如何透過測驗研究孩童的智商。
三、文意選填 第 31～40 題	改寫自 Coral Reef（珊瑚礁），描述珊瑚礁目前所遭受的各種威脅，以 及其重要性。
四、閱讀測驗 第 41～44 題	改寫自 From humble tool to global icon（從卑微的工具到全球品 牌），描述瑞士軍刀如何從士兵的工具變成世界知名品牌。
第 45～48 題	改寫自 Trash…..In Space?（外太空的垃圾？），描述若垃圾丟到外太 空，可能產生的問題。
第 49～52 題	改寫自 Neuroscience For Kids（孩童的神經科學），描述酒精測試的 方法及過程。
第 53～56 題	改寫自 Why do Indians have red dots?（為何印度人有紅點？），描述 印度女性眉心紅點的宗教意涵，及相關歷史。

【102 年學測】綜合測驗：16-20 出題來源

—— http://en.wikipedia.org/wiki/Telephone_numbering_plan

Telephone Numbering Plan

Area codes are also known as Numbering Plan Area (NPA) codes and formerly known as Subscriber trunk dialling (STD) codes in the UK. These are typically necessary only when dialed from outside the code area, from mobile phones, and, especially within North America, from within overlay plans. Area codes usually indicate geographical areas within one country that are covered by perhaps hundreds of telephone exchanges, although the correlation to geographical area is becoming obsolete.

The area code is usually preceded in the dial string by either the national access code ("0" for many countries, "1" in USA and Canada) or the international access code and country code. However, this is not always the case, especially when 10-digit dialing is used. For example, in Montreal, where area codes 514, 438, 450 and 579 are in use, users dial 10-digit number (e.g. 514 555 1234), dialing a 1 before this results in a recording advising not to dial a 1 as it is a local call. For non-geographic numbers, as well as mobile telephones outside of the North American Numbering Plan area, the "area code" does not correlate to a particular geographic area. However, until the 1990s, some areas in the United States required the use of a "1" before dialing a 7-digit number within the same area code if the call was beyond the local area, indicating that the caller wished to make what was referred to as a "toll call."

Area codes are often quoted including the national access code, for example a number in London: 020 8765 4321. Users must then correctly interpret the "020" as the code for London. If they call from another number in London, they merely dial 8765 4321, or if dialing from another country, drop the "0" and dial: +44 20 8765 4321.

⋮

【102 年學測】綜合測驗：21-25 出題來源

——http://www.fleur-de-coin.com/articles/coin-value

Determine the Value of a Coin

How much is my coin worth?

Many collectors have come across a particular coin from time to time and wondered whether they had something of great value in their possession. As a matter of fact the age old question "How much is this coin worth?" is probably the most frequently asked question about coins by non-collectors today. In order to assess what your coins are worth, you have to take into account a number of factors or even seek advice from experienced coin collectors. Remember, however, that the mere fact that a coin does not have significant monetary value does not mean that it is not interesting or that it should not form part of your collection.

The factors influencing the value of a coin are the following: rarity, demand, supply, age, condition, and other external factors. Any of these factors can be significant in itself, or it may require some help from one of the other factors. A coin could be common in low grades, indicating a low rarity, but very rare in high grades making it what is called a condition rarity. In such a case, the value of the coin makes a great jump in price as it moves from a lower grade to a higher grade.

Age

Age doesn't always increase the value of a coin. It actually has little effect on it, as there are many coins from the last 20 years or so that are much more valuable than coins from 2,000 years ago. For example, given the choice between a 2,000 year old Roman denarius or a U.S. $20 Gold piece, most non-numismatists will pick the Roman coin as being worth more. Hoever, the U.S. $20 Gold piece is worth considerably more than the Roman denarius.

⋮

【102年學測】綜合測驗：26-30 出題來源
——http://www.pbs.org/wgbh/aso/databank/entries/dh05te.html

A Science Odyssey: People and Discoveries

Binet pioneers intelligence testing 1905

French psychologist Alfred Binet (1859-1911) took a different tack than most psychologists of his day: he was interested in the workings of the normal mind rather than the pathology of mental illness. He wanted to find a way to measure the ability to think and reason, apart from education in any particular field.

In 1905 he developed a test in which he had children do tasks such as follow commands, copy patterns, name objects, and put things in order or arrange them properly. He gave the test to Paris schoolchildren and created a standard based on his data. For example, if 70 percent of 8-year-olds could pass a particular test, then success on the test represented the 8-year-old level of intelligence. From Binet's work, the phrase "intelligence quotient," or "IQ," entered the vocabulary. The IQ is the ratio of "mental age" to chronological age, with 100 being average. So, an 8 year old who passes the 10 year-old's test would have an IQ of 10/8 x 100, or 125.

Binet's work set off a passion for testing and in the enthusiasm, a widespread application of tests and scoring measures developed from relatively limited data. Tests based on Binet's test were used by the U.S. Army in sorting out the vast numbers of recruits in World War I. The questions, however, had much more to do with general knowledge than with mental tasks such as sequencing or matching. The results, released after the war, showed that the majority of recruits had a juvenile intelligence. This shocking news played into the hands ofeugenicists who argued that intelligence was an innate, inheritable trait limited to certain types (or nationalities) of people.

【102 年學測】文意選填：31-40 出題來源

——http://en.wikipedia.org/wiki/Coral_reef

Coral Reef

Coral reefs are underwater structures made from calcium carbonate secreted bycorals. Coral reefs are colonies of tiny animals found in marine waters that contain few nutrients. Most coral reefs are built from stony corals, which in turn consist of polypsthat cluster in groups. The polyps are like tiny sea anemones, to which they are closely related. Unlike sea anemones, coral polyps secrete hard carbonate exoskeletons which support and protect their bodies. Reefs grow best in warm, shallow, clear, sunny and agitated waters.

Often called "rainforests of the sea," coral reefs form some of the most diverseecosystems on Earth. They occupy less than 0.1% of the world's ocean surface, about half the area of France, yet they provide a home for 25% of all marine species, including fish, mollusks, worms, crustaceans, echinoderms, sponges, tunicates and other cnidarians. Paradoxically, coral reefs flourish even though they are surrounded by ocean waters that provide few nutrients. They are most commonly found at shallow depths in tropical waters, but deep water and cold water corals also exist on smaller scales in other areas.

Coral reefs deliver ecosystem services to tourism, fisheries and shoreline protection. The annual global economic value of coral reefs has been estimated at US$ 375 billion. However, coral reefs are fragile ecosystems, partly because they are very sensitive to water temperature. They are under threat from climate change, oceanic acidification,blast fishing, cyanide fishing for aquarium fish, overuse of reef resources, and harmful land-use practices, including urban and agricultural runoff and water pollution, which can harm reefs by encouraging excess algal growth.

⋮

【102 年學測】閱讀測驗：41-44 出題來源

——http://news.bbc.co.uk/2/hi/europe/8172917.stm

From humble tool to global icon

In Switzerland, there is a saying that every good Swiss citizen has one in his or her pocket.

It is an object that is recognised all over the world, and it is globally popular.

But the Swiss army knife had humble beginnings, and, at the start, it wasn't even red.

In the late 19th Century, the Swiss army issued its soldiers with a gun which required a special screwdriver to dismantle and clean it.

At the same time, tinned food was becoming common in army rations. Swiss generals decided to issue each soldier with a standard knife.

It was a life-saver for Swiss knife makers, who were, at the time, struggling to compete with cheaper German imports.

"My great-grandfather started a small business in 1884, 125 years ago," explains Carl Elsener, head of the Swiss knife manufacturer Victorinox.

"He was making knives for farmers, for in the kitchen and so on, and then he heard that the Swiss army wanted a knife for every Swiss soldier."

Carl Elsener senior seized that opportunity with both hands, and designed a knife that the army loved.

"It was a very simple thing," explains his great-grandson. "It had a black handle, one big blade, a tin opener and a screwdriver."
Global cult object

Now, to mark the 125th anniversary, that first knife is on display at an exhibition at the Forum for Swiss History, together with hundreds of other Swiss army knives.

⋮

【102 年學測】閱讀測驗：45-48 出題來源

——http://www.dogonews.com/2012/3/19/trashin-space/page/3

Trash……In Space?

Space is where our future is—Trips to the Moon, Mars and beyond. Most people would think that aside from a few meteors, asteroids, planets, comets and stars there is little else to stand in our way. But, over the last 55 years as humans have been venturing out in space they have left so many debris that scientists are now concerned that if we don't do something to clean it up, we may all be in mortal danger.

The first piece of space junk was created by mistake in 1964, when the connection with the American satellite Vanguard 1 was lost. However, since it kept rotating around the earth's orbit without any consequences, scientists became increasingly comfortable abandoning things that had outlived their use.

According to NASA, there are currently over 500,000 pieces of man-made trash orbiting the earth at speeds of up to 17,500 miles per hour. The debris vary from tiny flecks of paint chipped off of rockets to huge satellites and fuel tanks and even, odd items like the million dollar tool kit that NASA astronaut *Heidemarie Stefanyshyn Piper* lost, whilst on a space walk.

⋮

【102 年學測】閱讀測驗：49-52 出題來源
——http://faculty.washington.edu/chudler/ener.html

Alcohol, Energy Drinks and Breath Testing

Did you know that many popular energy drinks contain ALCOHOL? They do! Even those drinks that are supposed to be "non-alcoholic." In fact, some people who have tested positive on an alcohol breath test have claimed that they only drank a "non-alcoholic" energy drink. Can one of these energy drinks really cause someone to test positive on an alcohol breath test? Researchers in Missouri set up an experiment to find out.

First, the amount of alcohol in 27 different energy drinks was measured. The drinks tested included Red Bull, Full Throttle, andRockstar. All but one drink had a detectable alcohol level (greater than 0.005%). In 13 of the 27 drinks, the alcohol concentration was above 0.06% and in 9 of the 27 drinks, the alcohol concentration was at least 0.096%. (NOTE: In the United States, if the amount of alcohol in a drink is less than 0.5%, it does not have to be listed on the label.)

Although the amount of alcohol in the tested energy drinks was very low, the scientists investigated the possibility that these small levels of alcohol could be detected by a breath test. They asked test subjects to drink a full can or bottle of an energy drink and then gave each subject an alcohol breath test 1 minute and 15 minutes after the drink was finished.

⋮

【102 年學測】閱讀測驗：53-56 出題來源

——http://www.whycenter.com/why-do-indians-have-red-dots/

Why do Indians have red dots?

The majority of Indian women put a red dot between their eyebrows. The red dots signify their martial status—married women put a red dot, while unmarried girls put a small black dot on their forehead. The practice of putting a red dot on the forehead is primarily related to Hindu mythology.

It is believed that after marriage, the primary duty of the woman is to take care of her kin and kith. The red dot, in one hand, symbolizes the good fortune of a married woman, and on the other hand, it reminds her to uphold the sanctity of marriage. At one point of time, every married woman used to religiously follow this norm. However, with the passage of time, the thinking of people has changed dramatically. In the present day, women are educated and financially independent. Some of them do stringently follow the tradition, but for most of them, putting a red dot has become more of a fashion statement rather than a religious custom. Apart from red dot, women prefer the wear dots of different colors and styles, depending upon theirclothing.

⋮

The red dot also helps the Hindu woman or stand out in the crowd. In India, every religion is associated with some characteristic features. For instance, Muslim women compulsorily cover their face with a veil whenever they venture out. Likewise, the red dot on the forehead of a woman denotes that she is a Hindu.

In addition to women, Indian men also wear red dot. Again, this tradition is purely related to Hindu religious beliefs. Normally, after the performance of some rituals or religious ceremonies, the red dot is put on the forehead of men. Also, during festivals like Holi, Diwali, Dusshera and Raksha Bandhan, Indian men wear a red dot on their forehead. Whenever, men go for a long voyage or setup a new business venture or kick-start an important campaign, then too the red dot is placed on their forehead as a mark of good luck.

Priests, monks and saints also put a red dot on their forehead. It is believed that between the eyebrows is present the Ajna Chakra or the third eye, which is the center of spiritual energy. It is also called the Guru's (teacher) seat. By putting a red dot at this point, the monks and priests pay respect to their Guru, and seek their blessings to activate the Chakra and overcome the inner ego.

102 年學測英文科非選擇題閱卷評分原則說明

閱卷召集人：劉慶剛（國立台北大學應用外語學系教授）

102 學年度學科能力測驗英文考科的非選擇題題型共有「中譯英」和「英文作文」兩大題。第一大題是「中譯英」，題型與過去幾年相同，考生需將兩個中文句子譯成正確、通順、達意的英文，兩題合計為 8 分。第二大題是「英文作文」，考生須從三幅連環圖片的內容，想像第四幅圖片可能的發展，再以至少 120 個單詞寫出一個涵蓋連環圖片內容並有完整結局的故事。

關於閱卷籌備工作，依循閱卷標準程序，於 1 月 30 日先召開評分標準訂定會議，由正、副召集人及協同主持人共 14 人，參閱了約 3,000 份來自不同地區的試卷，經過一整天的討論之後，訂定評分標準，選出合適的評分參考樣卷及試閱樣卷，編製成閱卷參考手冊，供閱卷委員共同參閱。

2 月 1 日上午 9：00 到 11：00 召開試閱會議，166 位大學教授與會，首先由召集人說明評分標準；接著分組進行試閱，根據閱卷參考手冊的試閱樣卷分別評分，並討論評分準則，務求評分標準一致，確保閱卷品質。為求慎重，試閱會議之後，正、副召集人及協同主持人進行評分標準再確定會議，確認評分原則後才開始正式閱卷。

評分標準與歷年相同，在「中譯英」部分，每小題總分 4 分，原則上是每個錯誤扣 0.5 分。「英文作文」的評分標準是依據內容、組織、文法句構、詞彙拼字、體例五個項目給分，

字數明顯不足的作文則扣總分 1 分。閱卷時，每份試卷皆會經過兩位委員分別評分，最後成績以二位閱卷委員給分之平均成績爲準。如果第一閱與第二閱分數差距超過差分標準，將再由第三位委員（正、副召集人或協同主持人）評閱。

今年的「中譯英」與「高房價」有關，評量的重點在於考生能否能運用熟悉的詞彙與基本句型將中文翻譯成正確達意的英文句子，所測驗之句型爲高中生熟悉的範圍，詞彙亦控制在大考中心詞彙表四級內之詞彙，中等程度以上的考生，如果能使用正確句型並注意用字、拼字，應能得理想的分數。比如說，「都會區的高房價」若譯出 high house prices in city areas 即可得分；「對社會的嚴重影響」則可翻譯爲 serious effects on society。在選取樣卷時，我們發現有不少考生對於英文詞彙的使用及英文拼字仍有加強的空間，如第二句的「政府」和「政策」看起來是簡單的字，但有不少同學拼錯了，例如：government 少了中間的字母 n，policy 寫成 police 等，也有人把 satisfy 寫成 satisefy。

今年的「英文作文」主題與考生的生活經驗息息相關，大部分的考生應有不錯的發揮。根據作答提示，考生必須根據三幅連環圖片的內容，想像第四幅「空白圖片」可能的發展，寫出一個涵蓋連環圖片內容並有完整結局的故事，文長至少 120 個單詞。評分的考量重點爲作文內容應切題，組織具連慣性、句子結構及用字適切、拼字與標點符號的使用正確得當。

102 年學測英文科試題或答案之反映意見回覆

※ 題號：1

【題目】

1. It rained so hard yesterday that the baseball game had to be
＿＿＿＿＿＿ until next Saturday.
(A) surrendered　　　　(B) postponed
(C) abandoned　　　　(D) opposed

【意見內容】

選項 (C) abandoned 作「放棄」解釋時，應為合理選項。

【大考中心意見回覆】

Longman Dictionary of Contemporary English 的解釋，abandon 的定義是 to stop doing something because there are too many problems and it is impossible to continue。根據本試題題意，評量的是rain 與postpone the baseball game 之間的語意因果關係 (so…that…)，作答線索在空格後 …until next Saturday。選項 (C) abandoned 一詞與題幹until next Saturday 訊息不符，因此，選項 (C) 非正答選項。

※ 題號：6

【題目】

6. The bank tries its best to attract more customers. Its staff members are always available to provide ＿＿＿＿＿＿ service.
(A) singular　　　　(B) prompt
(C) expensive　　　　(D) probable

【意見內容】

1. 銀行外匯、放款、信託業務等幾乎都是個別的服務，尤其現在為了吸引更多的顧客，推出網路銀行提供個別的服務，因此選項 (A) singular 應為合理選項。再者，根據字典字義的解釋，選項 (A) 亦可作為合理選項。

2. 選項 (D) probable 作「可能的」解釋，應為合理選項。

【大考中心意見回覆】

1. 詞彙題的評量重點在於考生能否根據題幹說明，找出最符合題意的選項。本題的作答線索為題幹中 always available 與 prompt service 之間的語意關係。singular service 一詞在特定的情況下可用，但就本題題幹上下文（context），尤其是有 always（經常性）存在與對應的「語意」來觀照，prompt 是唯一「最適當」的答案。

2. probable 一詞的字義應該是「概率的、機率的」意思，並非作為「有可能的」解釋，與 possible 的意思不一樣，因此根據第六題題幹語意，選項 (D) probable 的字詞與題幹題意不符。

※ 題號：7

【題目】

7. John's part-time experience at the cafeteria is good _____ for running his own restaurant.
   (A) preparation   (B) recognition
   (C) formation   (D) calculation

【意見內容】

選項 (C) formation 應為答案。

【大考中心意見回覆】

本題評量考生掌握 …preparation for… 的慣用語用法，考生除了需要掌握 preparation 的語意之外，空格後的介系詞 for 是另一個作答線索。formation 不可與 for 搭配使用，且與題幹語意不符，因此選項 (C) formation 非正答選項。

※ 題號：**9**

【題目】

9. Standing on the seashore, we saw a _____ of seagulls flying over the ocean before they glided down and settled on the water.
   (A) pack
   (B) flock
   (C) herd
   (D) school

【意見內容】

選項 (C) herd 應為答案。

【大考中心意見回覆】

本題評量 a flock of 的搭配語用法。考生必須了解並掌握 a flock of seagulls 的用法；空格後的 seagulls 是作答線索。選項 (C) herd 一詞指的是圈養在一起的動物（比如：牛、羊等），海鷗並不屬於此類之動物，因此非本題正答選項。

※ 題號：**17**

【題目】

An area code is a section of a telephone number which generally represents the geographical area that the phone receiving the call is based in. It is the two or three digits just before the local number. If the number ___16___ is in the same area as the number making the call, an area code usually doesn't need to be dialed. The local number, ___17___, must always be dialed in its entirety.

The area code was introduced in the United States in 1947. It was created ___18___ the format of XYX, with X being any number between 2-9 and Y being either 1 or 0. Cities and areas with higher populations would have a smaller first and third digit, and 1 as the center digit. New York, being the largest city in the United States, was ___19___ the 212 area code, followed by Los Angeles at 213.

In countries other than the United States and Canada, the area code generally determines the ___20___ of a call. Calls within an area code and often a small group of neighboring area codes are normally charged at a lower rate than outside the area code.

17. (A) in fact　　　　　　　(B) to illustrate
　　(C) at the same time　　(D) on the other hand

【意見內容】

選項 (C) at the same time 比較有轉折的語氣，應為合理選項。

【大考中心意見回覆】

本題評量的是掌握連貫標記 on the other hand 在篇章中的用法。空格前一句 an area code usually doesn't need to be dialed 與後一句 The local number…must always be dialed in its entirety 之語意呈現對比關係，因此選項 (C) at the same time 非正答選項。

※ 題號：18

【題目】

An area code is a section of a telephone number which generally represents the geographical area that the phone receiving the call is based in. It is the two or three digits just before the local number. If the number ___16___ is in the same area as the number making the call, an area code usually doesn't need to be dialed. The local number, ___17___, must always be dialed in its entirety.

The area code was introduced in the United States in 1947. It was created ___18___ the format of XYX, with X being any number between 2-9 and Y being either 1 or 0. Cities and areas with higher populations would have a smaller first and third digit, and 1 as the center digit. New York, being the largest city in the United States, was ___19___ the 212 area code, followed by Los Angeles at 213.

In countries other than the United States and Canada, the area code generally determines the ___20___ of a call. Calls within an area code and often a small group of neighboring area codes are normally charged at a lower rate than outside the area code.

18. (A) for　　　(B) as　　　(C) by　　　(D) in

【意見內容】

選項 (C) by 應為合理選項。

【大考中心意見回覆】

本題評量的是掌握慣用語 in the format 在篇章中的用法。空格後 …the format of XYX, with X being any number between 2-9 and Y being either 1 or 0；而動詞被動式之後若接 by，則標示其後為動作之主事者（agent），亦即「area code 乃是被 XYX 的形式所創造」，顯與此處上下文意不符，因此選項 (C) by 非本題正答選項。

※ 題號：**19**

【題目】

An area code is a section of a telephone number which generally represents the geographical area that the phone receiving the call is based in. It is the two or three digits just before the local number. If the number ___16___ is in the same area as the number making the call, an area code usually doesn't need to be dialed. The local number, ___17___, must always be dialed in its entirety.

The area code was introduced in the United States in 1947. It was created ___18___ the format of XYX, with X being any number between 2-9 and Y being either 1 or 0. Cities and areas with higher populations would have a smaller first and third digit, and 1 as the center digit. New York, being the largest city in the United States, was ___19___ the 212 area code, followed by Los Angeles at 213.

In countries other than the United States and Canada, the area code generally determines the ___20___ of a call. Calls within an area code and often a small group of neighboring area codes are normally charged at a lower rate than outside the area code.

19. (A) reserved　　　　　　　(B) assigned
　　(C) represented　　　　　(D) assembled

【意見內容】

選項 (C) represented 應為合理選項。

【大考中心意見回覆】

本題評量詞彙 assigned 在篇章中的意義和用法。作答線索在空格前一句 Cities and areas with higher populations would have a smaller first and third digit, and 1 as the center digit. 及本句 New York, being the largest city in the United States, was…the 212 area code… 之語意關係。

assign 為雙賓動詞（與 give 同類，如 to give NP1 NP2, to assign NP1 NP2），而根據本句句意和文法結構，New York 為原主動句式之間接賓語(NP1)，空格後之名詞 the 212 area code 則為其直接賓語 (NP2)。而 represent 並非雙賓動詞，其被動式之後不能再接其他名詞片語做為賓語，因此語意及文法均不正確，因此選項 (C) represented 非正答選項。

※ 題號：**26**

【題目】

　　French psychologist Alfred Binet (1859-1911) took a different approach from most other psychologists of his day: He was interested in the workings of the ___26___ mind rather than the nature of mental illness. He wanted to find a way to measure the ability to think and reason, apart from education in any particular field. In 1905 he developed a test in which he ___27___ children do tasks such as follow commands, copy patterns, name objects, and put things in order or arrange them properly. He later created a standard of measuring children's intelligence ___28___ the data he had collected from the French children he studied. If 70 percent of 8-year-olds could pass a particular test, then ___29___ on the test represented an 8-year-old's level of intelligence. From Binet's work, the phrase "intelligence quotient" ("IQ") entered the English vocabulary. The IQ is the ratio of "mental age" to chronological age times 100, with 100 ___30___ the average. So, an 8-year-old who passes the 10-year-old's test would have an IQ of 10/8 times 100, or 125.

26. (A) contrary　　　　　　(B) normal
　　(C) detective　　　　　 (D) mutual

【意見內容】

　　選項 (C) detective 應為答案。

【大考中心意見回覆】

　　本題評量詞彙 normal 在篇章中的語意及用法。作答線索在空格前 ...the workings of ... mind 和空格後 ...rather than the nature of

mental illness 之語意，尤其是 rather than 暗示前後的語意應是對
比關係，因此只有選項 (B) normal 才符合本句語意。

※ 題號：27

【題目】

French psychologist Alfred Binet (1859-1911) took a different
approach from most other psychologists of his day: He was
interested in the workings of the ___26___ mind rather than the
nature of mental illness.　He wanted to find a way to measure the
ability to think and reason, apart from education in any particular
field.　In 1905 he developed a test in which he ___27___ children
do tasks such as follow commands, copy patterns, name objects,
and put things in order or arrange them properly.　He later created
a standard of measuring children's intelligence ___28___ the data he
had collected from the French children he studied.　If 70 percent
of 8-year-olds could pass a particular test, then ___29___ on the test
represented an 8-year-old's level of intelligence.　From Binet's
work, the phrase "intelligence quotient" ("IQ") entered the English
vocabulary.　The IQ is the ratio of "mental age" to chronological
age times 100, with 100 ___30___ the average.　So, an 8-year-old
who passes the 10-year-old's test would have an IQ of 10/8 times
100, or 125.

27. (A) had
　　(C) wanted
　　(B) kept
　　(D) asked

【意見內容】

選項 (D) asked 應為合理選項。

【大考中心意見回覆】

本題測驗詞彙 had 的使役動詞用法。作答線索在空格後...children do tasks such as follow commands, copy patterns, name objects, and put things in order or arrange them properly 之語意及該句中 do、copy、put 三個字詞皆為原形動詞，因此空格中必須填入使役動詞 had 一詞。若使用選項 (D) asked，則後面的動詞應為不定詞用法（to + 原形動詞），因此選項 (D) asked 非本題正答選項。

※ 題號：**29**

【題目】

　　French psychologist Alfred Binet (1859-1911) took a different approach from most other psychologists of his day: He was interested in the workings of the ___26___ mind rather than the nature of mental illness. He wanted to find a way to measure the ability to think and reason, apart from education in any particular field. In 1905 he developed a test in which he ___27___ children do tasks such as follow commands, copy patterns, name objects, and put things in order or arrange them properly. He later created a standard of measuring children's intelligence ___28___ the data he had collected from the French children he studied. If 70 percent of 8-year-olds could pass a particular test, then ___29___ on the test represented an 8-year-old's level of intelligence. From Binet's work, the phrase "intelligence quotient" ("IQ") entered the English vocabulary. The IQ is the ratio of "mental age" to chronological age times 100, with 100 ___30___ the average. So, an 8-year-old who passes the 10-year-old's test would have an IQ of 10/8 times 100, or 125.

29. (A) success　　　　　　　　(B) objection
　　(C) agreement　　　　　　　(D) discovery

【意見內容】

1. 原本第 29 題空格後之 an 8-year-old's level 應為 the 8-year-old's level 較為合適；而 From Binet's work, the phrase "intelligence quotinet"("IQ") entered the English vocabulary. 不合英文語法，原文所用的句子 Following Binet's work, the phrase "intelligence quotinet"("IQ") entered the English vocabulary. ，"following" 做為「由於」解釋，較符合文意。本題應不予計分。

2. 根據字典的字詞解釋，選項 (C) agreement 應為合理選項。

3. 選項 (B) objection 應為答案。

【大考中心意見回覆】

1. 空格後文字…an 8-year-old's level of intelligence 的 an 雖與原文使用的 the 不同，但因英文中的 an、a、the 皆可做為 generic（全部）使用，故在解讀與作答上並不會造成困難，因為本題之作答線索在於空格前的句子 If 70 percent of 8-year-olds could pass a particular test 與空格後的 …on the test represented an 8-year-old's level of intelligence 之語意連貫關係。再者，From Binet's work, the phrase "intelligence quotinet"("IQ") entered the English vocabulary. 之句構及語法並無不妥，亦不影響考生作答。

2. 選項 (C) agreement 語意無法與空格後的 on the test represented… 搭配使用，因為其語意將變成「對該測驗的意見/看法一致」，而非指測驗的結果。若要使用 agreement 一詞則可能需要加上 of the test results 等字詞較符合語法。

3. 本題之作答線索在於空格前的句子 If 70 percent of 8-year-olds could pass a particular test 與空格後的 …on the test represented

an 8-year-old's level of intelligence 之語意連貫關係。以英文一般常見的用法，didn't pass an exam 是 failure，pass a test 也就與 success on the test 密切呼應。選項 (B) objection 與文意發展不符，因此非本題正答。

※ 題號：30

【題目】

French psychologist Alfred Binet (1859-1911) took a different approach from most other psychologists of his day: He was interested in the workings of the ___26___ mind rather than the nature of mental illness. He wanted to find a way to measure the ability to think and reason, apart from education in any particular field. In 1905 he developed a test in which he ___27___ children do tasks such as follow commands, copy patterns, name objects, and put things in order or arrange them properly. He later created a standard of measuring children's intelligence ___28___ the data he had collected from the French children he studied. If 70 percent of 8-year-olds could pass a particular test, then ___29___ on the test represented an 8-year-old's level of intelligence. From Binet's work, the phrase "intelligence quotient" ("IQ") entered the English vocabulary. The IQ is the ratio of "mental age" to chronological age times 100, with 100 ___30___ the average. So, an 8-year-old who passes the 10-year-old's test would have an IQ of 10/8 times 100, or 125.

30. (A) is   (B) are   (C) been   (D) being

【意見內容】

選項 (C) been 應為答案。

【大考中心意見回覆】

本題測驗分詞片語 with…being 之句法結構。空格前 The IQ is the ratio of "mental age" to chronological age times 100…，以及空格後 with 100… the average 之分詞片語結構。選項 (C) been 與此處文法及語意均不符。

※ 題號：42

【題目】

The Swiss army knife is a popular device that is recognized all over the world. In Switzerland, there is a saying that every good Swiss citizen has one in his or her pocket. But the knife had humble beginnings.

In the late nineteenth century, the Swiss army issued its soldiers a gun that required a special screwdriver to dismantle and clean it. At the same time, canned food was becoming common in the army. Swiss generals decided to issue each soldier a standard knife to serve both as a screwdriver and a can opener.

It was a lifesaver for Swiss knife makers, who were struggling to compete with cheaper German imports. In 1884, Carl Elsener, head of the Swiss knife manufacturer Victorinox, seized that opportunity with both hands, and designed a soldier's knife that the army loved. It was a simple knife with one big blade, a can opener, and a screwdriver.

A few years after the soldier's knife was issued, the "Schweizer Offizier Messer," or Swiss Officer's Knife, came on the market.

Interestingly, the Officer's Knife was never given to those serving in the army. The Swiss military purchasers considered the new model with a corkscrew for opening wine not "essential for survival," so officers had to buy this new model by themselves. But its special multi-functional design later launched the knife as a global brand. After the Second World War, a great number of American soldiers were stationed in Europe. And as they could buy the Swiss army knife at shops on military bases, they bought huge quantities of them. However, it seems that "Schweizer Offizier Messer" was too difficult for them to say, so they just called it the Swiss army knife, and that is the name it is now known by all over the world.

42. What does "It" in the third paragraph refer to?

(A) The Swiss army needed a knife for every soldier.

(B) Every good Swiss citizen had a knife in his pocket.

(C) Swiss knives were competing with imported knives.

(D) Canned food was becoming popular in the Swiss army.

【意見內容】

1. 根據文章內容，選項 (D) 應為合理選項。

2. 選項 (C) 應為答案。

【大考中心意見回覆】

本題測驗考生是否能解讀上下文中指代詞（it）的篇章功能。作答線索是第二段最後一句 Swiss generals decided to issue each soldier a standard knife to serve both as a screwdriver and a can opener.。根據文章結構，第二段最後一個句子是第二段文意的總結，而第三段第一個句子中的 It 所回指的是第二段的文意總結，因此，除了選項 (A) 外，其餘選項皆與文意發展不符，非合理選項。

102 年大學入學學科能力測驗試題
數學考科

第壹部分：選擇題（佔 60 分）

一、單選題（佔 30 分）

說明：第 1 題至第 6 題，每題有 5 個選項，其中只有一個是正確或最適當的
　　　選項，請畫記在答案卡之「選擇（填）題答案區」。各題答對者，
　　　得 5 分；答錯、未作答或畫記多於一個選項者，該題以零分計算。

1. 學校規定上學期成績需同時滿足以下兩項要求，才有資格參選模
　 範生。
　 一、國文成績或英文成績 70 分（含）以上；
　 二、數學成績及格。
　 已知<u>小文</u>上學期國文 65 分而且他不符合參選模範生資格。請問
　 下列哪一個選項的推論是正確的？
　 (1) <u>小文</u>的英文成績未達 70 分
　 (2) <u>小文</u>的數學成績不及格
　 (3) <u>小文</u>的英文成績 70 分以上但數學成績不及格
　 (4) <u>小文</u>的英文成績未達 70 分以上且數學不及格
　 (5) <u>小文</u>的英文成績未達 70 分或數學成績不及格

2. 令 $a = 2.6^{10} - 2.6^{9}$，$b = 2.6^{11} - 2.6^{10}$，$c = \dfrac{2.6^{11} - 2.6^{9}}{2}$。請選出正確
　 的大小關係。
　 (1) $a > b > c$　　　　　(2) $a > c > b$
　 (3) $b > a > c$　　　　　(4) $b > c > a$
　 (5) $c > b > a$

3. 袋子裡有 3 顆白球，2 顆黑球。由甲、乙、丙三人依序各抽取 1 顆球，抽取後不放回。若每顆球被取出的機會相等，請問在甲和乙抽到相同顏色球的條件下，丙抽到白球之條件機率為何？

   (1) $\frac{1}{3}$　　(2) $\frac{5}{12}$　　(3) $\frac{1}{2}$　　(4) $\frac{3}{5}$　　(5) $\frac{2}{3}$

4. 已知以下各選項資料的迴歸直線（最適合直線）皆相同且皆為負相關，請選出相關係數最小的選項。

   (1)
x	2	3	5
y	1	13	1

   (2)
x	2	3	5
y	3	10	2

   (3)
x	2	3	5
y	5	7	3

   (4)
x	2	3	5
y	9	1	5

   (5)
x	2	3	5
y	7	4	4

5. 將 24 顆雞蛋分裝到紅、黃、綠的三個籃子。每個籃子都要有雞蛋，且黃、綠兩個籃子裡都裝奇數顆。請選出分裝的方法數。

   (1) 55　　(2) 66　　(3) 132　　(4) 198　　(5) 253

6. 莎韻觀測遠方等速率垂直上升的熱氣球。在上午 10:00 熱氣球的仰角為 30°，到上午 10:00 仰角變成 34°。請利用下表判斷到上午 10:30 時，熱氣球的仰角最接近下列哪一個度數？

θ	30°	34°	39°	40°	41°	42°	43°
$\sin\theta$	0.500	0.559	0.629	0.643	0.656	0.669	0.682
$\cos\theta$	0.866	0.829	0.777	0.766	0.755	0.743	0.731
$\tan\theta$	0.577	0.675	0.810	0.839	0.869	0.900	0.933

   (1) 39°　　(2) 40°　　(3) 41°　　(4) 42°　　(5) 43°

二、多選題（佔30分）

說明：第7題至第12題，每題有5個選項，其中至少有一個是正確的選
項，請將正確選項畫記在答案卡之「選擇（填）題答案區」。
各題之選項獨立判定，所有選項均答對者，得5分；答錯1個選項
者，得3分；答錯2個選項者，得1分；答錯多於2個選項或所
有選項均未作答者，該題以零分計算。

7. 空設 n 為正整數，符號 $\begin{bmatrix} 1 & 1 \\ 0 & 2 \end{bmatrix}^n$ 代表矩陣 $\begin{bmatrix} 1 & 1 \\ 0 & 2 \end{bmatrix}$ 自乘 n 次。

令 $\begin{bmatrix} 1 & 1 \\ 0 & 2 \end{bmatrix}^n = \begin{bmatrix} a_n & b_n \\ c_n & d_n \end{bmatrix}$，請選出正確的選項。

(1) $a_2 = 1$ (2) a_1, a_2, a_3 為等比數列

(3) d_1, d_2, d_3 為等比數列   (4) b_1, b_2, b_3 為等差數列

(5) c_1, c_2, c_3 為等差數列

8. 設 $a > 1 > b > 0$，關於下列不等式，請選出正確的選項。

(1) $(-a)^7 > (-a)^9$ (2) $b^{-9} > b^{-7}$

(3) $\log_{10} \dfrac{1}{a} > \log_{10} \dfrac{1}{b}$ (4) $\log_a 1 > \log_b 1$

(5) $\log_a b \geq \log_b a$

9. 設 $a < b < c$。已知實係數多項式函數 $y = f(x)$ 的圖形為一開口向上
的拋物線，且與 x 軸交於 $(a,0)$、$(b,0)$ 兩點；實係數多項式函數
$y = g(x)$ 的圖形亦為一開口向上的拋物線，且跟 x 軸相交於 $(b,0)$、
$(c,0)$ 兩點。請選出 $y = f(x) + g(x)$ 的圖形可能的選項。

(1) 水平直線   (2) 和 x 軸僅交於一點的直線

(3) 和 x 軸無交點的拋物線   (4) 和 x 軸僅交於一點的拋物線

(5) 和 x 軸交於兩點的拋物線

10. 坐標平面上考慮兩點 $Q_1(1,0)$，$Q_2(-1,0)$。在下列各方程式的圖形中，請選出其上至少有一點 P 滿足內積 $\overrightarrow{PQ_1} \cdot \overrightarrow{PQ_2} < 0$ 的選項。

(1) $y = \dfrac{1}{2}$

(2) $y = x^2 + 1$

(3) $-x^2 + 2y^2 = 1$

(4) $4x^2 + y^2 = 1$

(5) $\dfrac{x^2}{2} - \dfrac{y^2}{2} = 1$

11. 設 F_1, F_2 為橢圓 Γ 的兩個焦點。S 為以 F_1 為中心的正方形（S 的各邊可不與 Γ 的對稱軸平行）。試問 S 可能有幾個頂點落在 Γ 上？

(1) 1

(2) 2

(3) 3

(4) 4

(5) 0

12. 設實數組成的數列 $\langle a_n \rangle$ 是公比為 -0.8 的等比數列，實數組成的數列 $\langle b_n \rangle$ 是首項為 10 的等差數列。已知 $a_9 > b_9$ 且 $a_{10} > b_{10}$。請選出正確的選項。

(1) $a_9 \times a_{10} < 0$

(2) $b_{10} > 0$

(3) $b_9 > b_{10}$

(4) $a_9 > a_{10}$

(5) $a_8 > b_8$

第貳部分：選填題（佔 40 分）

說明：1. 第 A 至 H 題，將答案畫記在答案卡之「選擇（填）題答案區」所標示的列號（13–35）。

2. 每題完全答對給 5 分，答錯不倒扣，未完全答對不給分。

A. 設 k 為一整數。已知 $\dfrac{k}{3} < \sqrt{31} < \dfrac{k+1}{3}$，則 $k =$ ___⑬⑭___ 。

B. 設 a, b 為實數且 $(a + bi)(2 + 6i) = -80$，其中 $i^2 = -1$。
則 $(a,b) = ($ ___⑮⑯___ , ___⑰⑱___ $)$ 。

C. 坐標平面中 $A(a,3)$, $B(16,b)$, $C(19,12)$ 三點共線。已知 C 不在 A, B 之間，且 $\overline{AB} : \overline{BC} = 3 : 1$，則 $a + b =$ ___⑲⑳___ 。

D. 阿德賣 100 公斤的香蕉，第一天每公斤賣 40 元；沒賣完的部份，第二天降價為每公斤 36 元。第三天再降為每公斤 32 元，到第三天全部賣完，三天所得共為 3720 元。假設阿德在第三天所賣香蕉的公斤數為 t，可算得第二天賣出香蕉的公斤數為 $at + b$，其中 $a =$ ___㉑㉒___ ， $b =$ ___㉓㉔___ 。

E. 坐標平面上，一圓與直線 $x - y = 1$ 以及直線 $x - y = 5$ 所截的弦長皆為 14。則此圓的面積為 ___㉕㉖___ π。

F. 令 $\vec{A}$, $\vec{B}$ 為坐標平面上兩向量。已知 $\vec{A}$ 的長度為 1，$\vec{B}$ 的長度為 2 且 $\vec{A}$ 與 $\vec{B}$ 之間的夾角為 $60°$。令 $\vec{u} = \vec{A} + \vec{B}$，$\vec{v} = x\vec{A} + y\vec{B}$，其中 x, y 為實數且符合 $6 \leq x + y \leq 8$ 以及 $-2 \leq x - y \leq 0$，則內積 $\vec{u} \cdot \vec{v}$ 的最大值為 ___㉗㉘___ 。

G. 設銳角三角形 *ABC* 的外接圓半徑為 8，已知外接圓圓心到 $\overline{AB}$ 的距離為 2，而到 $\overline{BC}$ 的距離為 7，則 $\overline{AC} = \underline{\;\;㉙\sqrt{㉚㉛}\;\;}$ 。
（化成最簡根式）

H. 如下圖，在坐標空間中，*A, B, C, D, E, F, G, H* 為正立方體的八個頂點，已知其中四個點的坐標 *A*(0,0,0)、*B*(6,0,0)、*D*(0,6,0) 及 *E*(0,0,6)，*P* 在線段 $\overline{CG}$ 上且 $\overline{CP}:\overline{PG}=1:5$，*R* 在線段 $\overline{EH}$ 上且 $\overline{ER}:\overline{RH}=1:1$，*Q* 在線段 $\overline{AD}$ 上。若空間中通過 *P, Q, R* 這三點的平面，與直線 *AG* 不相交，則 *Q* 點的 *y* 坐標為 $\dfrac{㉜㉝}{㉞㉟}$ 。
（化成最簡分數）

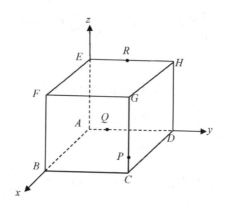

參考公式及可能用到的數值

1. 首項為 *a*，公差為 *d* 的等差數列前 *n* 項之和為 $S = \dfrac{n(2a_1 + (n-1)d)}{2}$

   首項為 *a*，公比為 *r* ($r \neq 1$) 的等比數列前 *n* 項之和為 $S_n = \dfrac{a(1-r^n)}{1-r}$，

2. 三角函數的和角公式：
$$\sin(A + B) = \sin A \cos B + \cos A \sin B$$
$$\cos(A + B) = \cos A \cos B - \sin A \sin B$$
$$\tan(A + B) = \frac{\tan A + \tan B}{1 - \tan A \tan B}$$

3. $\triangle ABC$ 的正弦定理：$\dfrac{a}{\sin A} = \dfrac{b}{\sin B} = \dfrac{c}{\sin C} = 2R$，

（ R 為 $\triangle ABC$ 的外接圓半徑）

$\triangle ABC$ 的餘弦定理：$c^2 = a^2 + b^2 - 2ab \cos C$

4. 一維數據 $X : x_1, x_2, \ldots, x_n$，

算術平均數：$\mu_X = \dfrac{1}{n}(x_1 + x_2 + \cdots + x_n) = \dfrac{1}{n}\sum_{i=1}^{n} x_i$

標準差：$\sigma_X = \sqrt{\dfrac{1}{n}\sum_{i=1}^{n}(x_i - \mu_X)^2} = \sqrt{\dfrac{1}{n}\left(\left(\sum_{i=1}^{n} x_i^2\right) - n{\mu_X}^2\right)}$

5. 二維數據 $(X, Y) : (x_1, y_1), (x_2, y_2), \ldots, (x_n, y_n)$，

相關係數 $r_{X,Y} = \dfrac{\sum_{i=1}^{n}(x_i - \mu_X)(y_i - \mu_Y)}{n\sigma_X \sigma_Y}$

迴歸直線（最適合直線）方程式 $y - \mu_Y = r_{X,Y} = \dfrac{\sigma_Y}{\sigma_X}(x - \mu_X)$

6. 參考數值：$\sqrt{2} \approx 1.414$，$\sqrt{3} \approx 1.732$，$\sqrt{5} \approx 2.236$，$\sqrt{6} \approx 2.449$，

$\pi \approx 3.142$

7. 對數值：$\log_{10} 2 \approx 0.3010$，$\log_{10} 3 \approx 0.4771$，$\log_{10} 5 \approx 0.6990$，

$\log_{10} 7 \approx 0.8451$

102年度學科能力測驗數學科試題詳解

第壹部分：選擇題

一、單選擇

1. 【答案】(5)

　　【解析】參選模範生的資格為：

　　　　　　(一) 國文成績或英文成績 70 分（含）以上

　　　　　　(二) 數學成績及格

　　　　　　兩項要求都要達成才行 ⇒ 只要 (一) 或 (二) 達不到就不符合參選模範生的資格

　　　　　　而小文上學期國文成績 65 分，卻不符合參選模範生的資格

　　　　　　∴ 小文英文成績未達 70 分（違反 (一)），或數學成績不及格（違反 (二)），故選 (5)

2. 【答案】(4)

　　【解析】$a = 2.6^{10} - 2.6^{9} = 2.6^{9}(2.6-1) = 2.6^{9} \times 1.6$

　　　　　　$b = 2.6^{11} - 2.6^{10} = 2.6^{10}(2.6-1) = 2.6^{10} \times 1.6 = 2.6^{9} \times 4.16$

　　　　　　$c = \dfrac{2.6^{11} - 2.6^{9}}{2} = \dfrac{2.6^{9}(2.6^{2}-1)}{2} = 2.6^{9} \times \dfrac{5.76}{2} = 2.6^{9} \times 2.88$

　　　　　　$\Rightarrow b > c > a$　　故選 (4)

3. 【答案】(3)

　　【解析】P（丙抽到白球｜甲和乙抽到相同顏色球）

$$= \frac{\dfrac{3}{5} \times \dfrac{2}{4} \times \dfrac{1}{3} + \dfrac{2}{5} \times \dfrac{1}{4} \times 1}{\dfrac{3}{5} \times \dfrac{2}{4} + \dfrac{2}{5} \times \dfrac{1}{4}} = \frac{1}{2} \qquad 故選 (3)$$

4. 【答案】(5)

   【解析】已知迴歸直線斜率相同，且為負相關，而 $m = r_{x,y} \times \dfrac{\sigma_Y}{\sigma_X}$

   由觀察知 σ_x 相同，得 $r_{x,y} \cdot \sigma_Y$ 為定值

   又 $r_{x,y} < 0$，在 σ_Y 最小時，$r_{x,y}$ 最小

   故只須找 σ_Y 最小即可，由 (1) 之 $\sigma_Y = 4\sqrt{2}$ ；

   (2) 之 $\sigma_Y = \sqrt{\dfrac{38}{3}}$ ；(3) 之 $\sigma_Y = \sqrt{\dfrac{8}{3}}$ ；(4) 之 $\sigma_Y = 4\sqrt{\dfrac{2}{3}}$ ；

   (5) 之 $\sigma_Y = \sqrt{2}$ （最小） 故選 (5)

5. 【答案】(2)

   【解析】設紅、黃、綠三個籃子各裝了 x、y、z 個雞蛋，

   得 $x + y + z = 24$

   其中 $x \geq 1$，y、z 皆為正奇數

   由 $y + z$ 必為偶數，得 $x = 24 - (y + z)$ 必為正偶數

   令 $x = 2x'+2 \geq 2$、$y = 2y'+1 \geq 1$、$z = 2z'+1 \geq 1$

   代入 $x + y + z = 24$

   $\Rightarrow (2x'+2) + (2y'+1) + (2z'+1) = 24 \Rightarrow x'+y'+z' = 10$

   有 $C_{10}^{3+10-1} = C_{10}^{12} = C_2^{12} = 66$ 種方法

【另解】 黃、綠籃子皆裝了正奇數個雞蛋，得紅籃子必裝正偶數
個雞蛋

紅	黃＋綠	（黃，綠）	方法數
22	2	（1，1）	1
20	4	（1，3）、（3，1）	2
18	6	（1，5）、（3，3）、（5，1）	3
⋮	⋮	⋯	⋮
2	22	（1，21）、（3，19）、⋯、（21，1）	11

共有 $1+2+3+\cdots+11 = \dfrac{(1+11)\times 11}{2} = 66$ 種　　故選 (2)

6. 【答案】 (3)

【解析】 如略圖，設觀測點與熱氣球在地面的投影點距離 x

由 10：10 時的仰角為 34°，

得熱氣球高度為 $x\tan 34^\circ = 0.675x$

得熱氣球每 10 分鐘上升

$0.675x - 0.577x = 0.098x$

故 10：30 時熱氣球高度為

$0.577x + 3\times 0.098x = 0.871x$

設 10：30 時熱氣球仰角 θ

得 $\tan\theta = \dfrac{0.871x}{x} = 0.871 \approx \tan 41^\circ$　　故選 (3)

二、多選題

7. 【答案】 (1) (2) (3) (5)

【解析】 $\begin{bmatrix} 1 & 1 \\ 0 & 2 \end{bmatrix} = \begin{bmatrix} a_1 & b_1 \\ c_1 & d_1 \end{bmatrix} \Rightarrow (a_1, b_1, c_1, d_1) = (1,1,0,2)$

$$\begin{bmatrix} 1 & 1 \\ 0 & 2 \end{bmatrix}^2 = \begin{bmatrix} 1 & 1 \\ 0 & 2 \end{bmatrix}\begin{bmatrix} 1 & 1 \\ 0 & 2 \end{bmatrix} = \begin{bmatrix} 1 & 3 \\ 0 & 4 \end{bmatrix} = \begin{bmatrix} a_2 & b_2 \\ c_2 & d_2 \end{bmatrix}$$

$$\Rightarrow (a_2, b_2, c_2, d_2) = (1,3,0,4)$$

$$\begin{bmatrix} 1 & 1 \\ 0 & 2 \end{bmatrix}^3 = \begin{bmatrix} 1 & 1 \\ 0 & 2 \end{bmatrix}^2\begin{bmatrix} 1 & 1 \\ 0 & 2 \end{bmatrix} = \begin{bmatrix} 1 & 3 \\ 0 & 4 \end{bmatrix}\begin{bmatrix} 1 & 1 \\ 0 & 2 \end{bmatrix}$$

$$= \begin{bmatrix} 1 & 7 \\ 0 & 8 \end{bmatrix} = \begin{bmatrix} a_3 & b_3 \\ c_3 & d_3 \end{bmatrix}$$

$$\Rightarrow (a_3, b_3, c_3, d_3) = (1,7,0,8)$$

(1) ○；$a_2 = 1$

(2) ○；$a_1 = a_2 = a_3 = 1 \Rightarrow a_2 - a_1 = a_3 - a_2 = 0$（公差），

故 a_1、a_2、a_3 爲等差數列

(3) ○；$\dfrac{d_2}{d_1} = \dfrac{d_3}{d_2} = 2$（公比），

故 d_1、d_2、d_3 爲等比數列

(4) ×；$b_1 = 1, b_2 = 3, b_3 = 7 \Rightarrow b_2 - b_1 = 2; b_3 - b_2 = 4$，

故 b_1、b_2、b_3 爲等比數列

(5) ○；$c_1 = c_2 = c_3 = 0 \Rightarrow c_2 - c_1 = c_3 - c_2 = 0$（公差），

故 c_1、c_2、c_3 爲等差數列

故選 (1) (2) (3) (5)

8. 【答案】(1) (2)

　　【解析】(1) ○；∵ $a > 1$ 且 $7 < 9 \Rightarrow 0 < a^7 < a^9$

　　　　　　　∴ $(-a)^7 = -a^7 > -a^9 = (-a)^9$

(2) ○；∵ $0<b<1$ 且 $-9<-7$　　∴ $b^{-9}>b^{-7}$

(3) ×；∵ $a>1>b>0$

∴ $0<\dfrac{1}{a}<\dfrac{1}{b} \Rightarrow \log_{10}\dfrac{1}{a}<\log_{10}\dfrac{1}{b}$

(4) ×；$\log_a 1=0=\log_b 1$

(5) ×；反例：設 $a=2>1>b=\dfrac{1}{4}>0$，

則 $\log_a b=\log_2 \dfrac{1}{4}=-2$，$\log_b a=\log_{\frac{1}{4}} 2=-\dfrac{1}{2}$

得 $\log_a b<\log_b a$　　　故選 (1) (2)

9. 【答案】(4) (5)

【解析】由題意可設 $y=f(x)=A(x-a)(x-b)$，$A>0$

$$y=g(x)=B(x-b)(x-c)，B>0$$

∴ $y=f(x)+g(x)=A(x-a)(x-b)+B(x-b)(x-c)$

$$=(A+B)(x-b)(x-\dfrac{Aa+Bc}{A+B}$$

圖形必為一開口向上的拋物線，且與 x 軸至少交一點

（ⅰ）當 $\dfrac{Aa+Bc}{A+B}=b$ 時

$y=f(x)+g(x)=(A+B)(x-b)^2$，圖形為與 x 軸恰

交一點之拋物線

（ⅱ）當 $\dfrac{Aa+Bc}{A+B}\neq b$ 時

$y=f(x)+g(x)=(A+B)(x-b)(x-\dfrac{Aa+Bc}{A+B})$，圖形

為與 x 軸恰交兩點之拋物線

故選 (4) (5)

10. 【答案】(1) (3) (4)

【解析】若 $\overrightarrow{PQ_1} \cdot \overrightarrow{PQ_2} = 0$，$P$ 點在以 $Q_1(1,0)$、$Q_2(-1,0)$ 為直徑兩

端點之圓 $x^2 + y^2 = 1$ 上

∵ $\overrightarrow{PQ_1} \cdot \overrightarrow{PQ_2} < 0$

∴ $\angle Q_1PQ_2 > 90°$，即知 P 點在圓 $x^2 + y^2 = 1$ 的內部

得知選項的圖形必須有部分的點要在圓 $x^2 + y^2 = 1$ 內部，

作圖如下

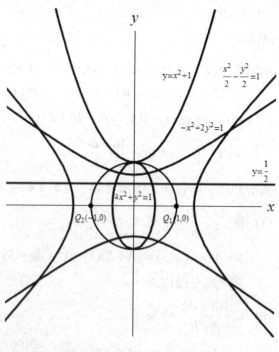

故選 (1) (3) (4)

11. 【答案】 (1) (2) (5)

　　【解析】 (1) ○ ；

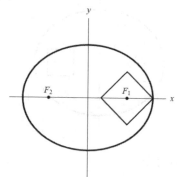

　　　　　(2) ○ ；

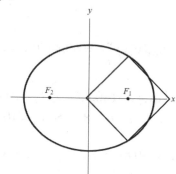

　　　　　(3) ×；橢圓 $\Gamma : \dfrac{x^2}{a^2} + \dfrac{y^2}{b^2} = 1$ 之一焦點 $F(c,0)$ ，

　　　　　　　若 $P(x_0, y_0)$ 在橢圓上，由橢圓的圖形之對稱性可

　　　　　　　知，最多只有兩個點 $P(x_0, y_0)$ 、 $Q(x_0 - y_0)$ 與焦點

　　　　　　　$F(c,0)$ 的距離相同，故不可能有超過 2 個頂點落

　　　　　　　在橢圓 Γ 上

　　　　　(4) ×；由 (3) 知

(5) ○；

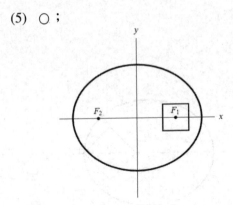

故選 (1) (2) (5)

12. 【答案】(1) (3)

【解析】(1) ○；由題意得 $\dfrac{a_{10}}{a_9} = -0.8 < 0 \Rightarrow a_9 \cdot a_{10} < 0$

(2) ×；$\begin{cases} a_9 = a_1 \cdot (-0.8)^8 \ > \ b_9 = 10 + 8d \cdots (1) \\ a_{10} = a_1 \cdot (-0.8)^9 \ > \ b_{10} = 10 + 9d \cdots (2) \end{cases}$

由 $(1) \times (-0.8) \Rightarrow a_{10} = a_1 \cdot (-0.8)^9 < (10 + 8d) \cdot (-0.8)$

$$= -8 - 6.4d$$

得 $10 + 9d < a_{10} < -8 - 6.4d \Rightarrow 15.4d < -18$

$$\Rightarrow d < \dfrac{-90}{77} < 0$$

$$\therefore b_{10} = 10 + 9d < 10 - \dfrac{810}{77} = -\dfrac{40}{77} < 0$$

(3) ○；由 (2) 知 $d < \dfrac{-90}{77} < 0 \Rightarrow b_9 > b_{10}$

(4) ×；若 $a_1 > 0 \Rightarrow a_9 > 0 > a_{10}$；

若 $a_1 < 0 \Rightarrow a_{10} > 0 > a_9$

(5)　$\times$；取 $a_1 = (\dfrac{5}{4})^7 \Rightarrow a_8 = -1$；

　　取 $d = -\dfrac{3}{2} \Rightarrow b_8 = 10 + 7 \times (-\dfrac{3}{2}) = -\dfrac{1}{2}$

　　得 $a_8 < b_8$　　　故選 (1) (3)

第貳部份：選填題

A. 【答案】16

　【解析】$\dfrac{k}{3} < \sqrt{31} < \dfrac{k+1}{3} \Rightarrow k^2 < 279 < (k+1)^2$

　　　　又 $16^2 = 256 < 279 < 17^2 = 289$　　　$\therefore k = 16$

B. 【答案】$(-4，12)$

　【解析】$(a+bi)(2+6i) = -80 \Rightarrow (2a-6b)+(6a+2b)i$

　　　　$= -80 \Rightarrow \left\{\begin{array}{l} 2a - 6b = -80 \\ 6a + 2b = 0 \end{array}\right\} \Rightarrow a = -4, b = 12$

C. 【答案】19

　【解析】由題意及分點公式得

　　　　$(16, b) = (\dfrac{1 \times a + 2 \times 19}{3}, \dfrac{1 \times 3 + 2 \times 12}{3})$

　　　　$= (\dfrac{a+38}{3}, 9)$

　　　　$\Rightarrow (a, b) = (10, 9)$

　　　　$\Rightarrow a + b = 10 + 9 = 19$

【另解】 由題意得 $\overrightarrow{CA} = 3\overrightarrow{CB} \Rightarrow (a-19, 3-12) = 3(16-19, b-12)$

$\Rightarrow (a-19, -9) = 3(-3, b-12) = (-9, 3b-36)$

$\Rightarrow (a, b) = (10, 9) \Rightarrow a+b = 10+9 = 19$

D. 【答案】 $(-2，70)$

【解析】 設第一天賣 x 公斤，第二天賣 y 公斤，第三天賣 t 公斤，則由題意知

$$\begin{cases} x+y+t = 100 \\ 40x+36y+32t = 3720 \end{cases} \Rightarrow \begin{cases} x+y+t = 100 \cdots (1) \\ 10x+9y+8t = 930 \cdots (2) \end{cases}$$

由 $(1) \times 10 - (2)$ 得 $y+2t = 70 \Rightarrow y = -2t+70$

$\therefore (a, b) = (-2, 70)$

E. 【答案】 51π

【解析】 由圓形知，圓心在直線 $x-y = 3$ 上

故圓心與直線 $x-y = 1$ 之距離為

$$\frac{|3-1|}{\sqrt{1^2 + (-1)^2}} = \sqrt{2}$$

得半徑 $r = \sqrt{(\sqrt{2})^2 + 7^2} = \sqrt{51}$

面積為 $A = r^2 \pi = 51\pi$

F. 【答案】 31

【解析】 $\vec{u} \cdot \vec{v} = (\vec{A}+\vec{B}) \cdot (x\vec{A}+y\vec{B}) = x|\vec{A}|^2 + y|\vec{B}|^2 + (x+y)\vec{A} \cdot \vec{B}$

$$= x \cdot 1^2 + y \cdot 2^2 + (x+y) \cdot 1 \cdot 2 \cdot \cos 60^\circ$$

$$= x + 4y + (x+y) = 2x + 5y$$

(x,y)	$2x + 5y$
$(2,4)$	24
$(3,5)$	31
$(4,4)$	28
$(3,3)$	21

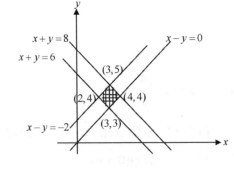

得最大值 31

G. 【答案】 $4\sqrt{15}$

【解析】 $\overline{BM} = \sqrt{8^2 - 2^2} = 2\sqrt{15}$ 、 $\overline{BN} = \sqrt{8^2 - 7^2} = \sqrt{15}$

得 $\cos\angle ABO = \dfrac{2\sqrt{15}}{8} = \dfrac{\sqrt{15}}{4} \Rightarrow \sin\angle ABO = \dfrac{1}{4}$

$\cos\angle CBO = \dfrac{\sqrt{15}}{8} \Rightarrow \sin\angle CBO = \dfrac{7}{8}$

$\therefore \sin\angle ABC = \sin(\angle ABO + \angle CBO)$

$$= \dfrac{1}{4} \times \dfrac{\sqrt{15}}{8} + \dfrac{\sqrt{15}}{4} \times \dfrac{7}{8}$$

$$= \dfrac{8\sqrt{15}}{4 \times 8} = \dfrac{\sqrt{15}}{4}$$

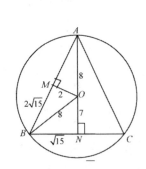

$$由正弦定理得 \frac{\overline{AC}}{\sin \angle ABC} = 2 \times 8 \Rightarrow \overline{AC} = 16 \sin \angle ABC$$

$$= 16 \times \frac{\sqrt{15}}{4} = 4\sqrt{15}$$

H. 【答案】 $\dfrac{15}{11}$

【解析】 由題意知 $P(6,6,1)$、$R(0,3,6)$

設 $Q(0,y,0)$

則平面 E_{PQR} 之法向量 $\vec{n}$ 滿足

$\vec{n} \mathbin{/\!/} \overrightarrow{PQ} \times \overrightarrow{PR} = (-6, y-6, -1) \times (-6, -3, 5)$

$= (5y-33, 36, 6y-18)$

又直線 $\overrightarrow{AG}$ 與平面 E_{PQR} 不相交，則

$\overrightarrow{AG} \mathbin{/\!/} E_{PQR} \Rightarrow \overrightarrow{AG} \cdot \vec{n} = 0$

$\Rightarrow (6,6,6) \cdot (5y-33, 36, 6y-18) = 0$

$\Rightarrow 11y - 15 = 0$

$\Rightarrow y = \dfrac{15}{11}$

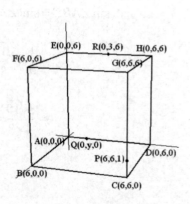

102 年大學入學學科能力測驗試題
社會考科

單選題（佔 144 分）

說明：第 1 題至第 72 題皆計分。每題有 4 個選項，其中只有一個是最
　　　正確或最適當的選項，請畫記在答案卡之「選擇題答案區」。
　　　各題答對者，得 2 分；答錯、未作答或畫記多於一個選項者，
　　　該題以零分計算。

1. 由於移民、移工和全球化潮流等因素，為現代社會帶來多元文化，
   使得國人與異文化的接觸增加。下列哪一種作法最有助於改善國
   人對異文化所產生的刻板印象？
   (A) 某電視台購買並播出外國的綜藝節目
   (B) 職棒聯盟邀請國外球隊來臺參與賽事
   (C) 臺灣某外商公司邀請國際巨星來臺演出
   (D) 國內外各大學締結姊妹校辦理學生交換

2. 人權是普世價值，許多國家都在相關法律中明文保障。以下關於
   人權的敘述何者正確？
   (A) 人權的實踐要考慮文化差異，有些國家的女性沒有投票權，
       這是文化差異，和人權無關
   (B) 學校規定不可以體罰，但家庭教育有體罰，且通常是為小孩
       好，故沒有侵犯人權的疑慮
   (C) 人權和公民權的範圍不同，來臺的外籍觀光客沒有公民權，
       但我國法律仍然保障其人權
   (D) 罪犯因為違反法律，而且往往對他人的人權造成侵害，因此
       國家不需要保障罪犯的人權

3. 甲報社報導：「策劃重大恐怖事件的中東恐怖組織領袖遭美國情報人員擊斃，對美國威望的提升以及未來的全球戰略均有重大意義……」；

　乙報社報導：「恐怖攻擊事件發生時，美國曾譴責中東國家是暴力分子，現在自己卻以暗殺的恐怖手段結束這位英雄的生命，令人遺憾……」。

　針對上述報導，下列何者是兩家報社對此事件做出迥異報導的最主要原因？

(A) 各家報社本就有其不同的立場

(B) 為擴大自家報社的市場占有率

(C) 為追求輿論的平衡而刻意不同

(D) 所有報導向來都無法呈現真相

4. 公共利益的推動，除了透過國家的公權力之外，也常經由公民團體的倡議。下列哪個例子屬於公民團體的倡議活動範疇？

(A) 網民串聯集結在總統府前廣場，要求政府肅貪反污

(B) 有志人士組成妓權團體，遊說政府將性工作除罪化

(C) 教授帶領一群學生，抗爭政府執行都市更新不公平

(D) 學者連署在報紙刊登廣告，呼籲政府重視失業問題

5. 關於自我發展的相關理論中，美國社會學家米德（George Herbert Mead）的論點備受重視，特別是他提出自我是由主我（I）與客我（me）構成的看法。針對其理論的敘述，下列何者正確？

(A) 因為主我的作用，個人習慣被動接受社會的規範

(B) 因為客我的作用，個人常常會表現出客觀和衝動

(C) 若個人的自我受主我的支配多一些，較具創造力

(D) 若主我與客我能和諧互動，個人的自我才能成長

6. 志願結社的蓬勃發展已經成為當代臺灣多元社會的特徵，透過志願結社，可以形成關心公共事務的社會文化，這正是民主政治蓬勃發展的基礎。下列關於志願結社的敘述何者最為正確？
   (A) 為民間所發起，但並不包含與政治關係密切的政黨
   (B) 必須向政府正式立案登記，否則結社行為不具效力
   (C) 強調公民直接參與公共事務，對政府採取抗爭立場
   (D) 強調非營利的性質，但仍可採取企業性經營或活動

7. 選舉制度對於民主國家的政治制度與政府運作具有關鍵性之影響。根據我國現行的選舉制度，下列敘述何者正確？
   (A) 總統選舉採取兩輪投票制，故不會產生支持度未能過半的總統
   (B) 縣市升格為直轄市後，市長的選舉改採單一選區絕對多數決制
   (C) 縣市議員選舉採取複數選區制，名額較多能兼顧地方多元聲音
   (D) 立法委員選舉採取絕對多數決制，故能充分代表地方主流意見

8. 公共政策制定過程中，政策合法化乃是一項政策提案取得法定地位的過程，從而使政策對社會產生拘束力並執行之。請問下列敘述何者最能代表政策合法化的內涵？
   (A) 地方政府針對石化產業投資案，完成設廠地點之環境影響報告
   (B) 苗栗縣經縣議會表決通過，同意由縣政府撥款舉辦元宵節燈會
   (C) 經濟部研擬提出「經濟動能推升方案」，據以促進經濟的發展
   (D) 衛生署完成「萊克多巴胺風險評估報告」，列入食品安全參考

9. 我國大陸政策制定過程中，1980 年代蔣經國總統曾提出「三不」政策，2000 年陳水扁總統曾表達「四不一沒有」的立場，2008 年馬英九總統就任後，也提出「新三不」的兩岸政策。關於前述「三不」、「四不」與「新三不」這三個政策或立場，以下敘述何者正確？

(A) 蔣總統的「三不」，已透露出其晚年企圖打破兩岸對立的現狀

(B) 陳總統的「四不」，堅持兩岸「一邊一國」漢賊不兩立的立場

(C) 馬總統的「新三不」，跟陳總統「四不」都有「不獨」的意涵

(D) 「四不」與「三不」基本上一樣，僅多出了「不會宣布獨立」

10. 某內閣制國家，有甲乙丙丁戊五個政黨，本次國會大選選舉結果
如表 1。依表中資訊判斷，下列有關其聯合內閣組成之敘述何者
正確？

表 1

政黨名稱	甲	乙	丙	丁	戊
國會席次	8	21	26	12	33

(A) 甲黨所獲得的席次過少，沒有參與組織聯合內閣的機會

(B) 丙黨若不想與過多政黨分享內閣權力，只能與戊黨合作

(C) 甲乙丁三黨過半，組成聯合內閣可以獲得國會穩定多數

(D) 乙丙兩黨若想合作組閣，只能夠尋求丁黨或戊黨的協助

11. 某重大貪瀆弊案遭揭發後，有公務人員接獲指示：「務必積極主動
擴大調查、證據蒐集齊全，將貪瀆集團成員一網打盡，並將貪污之
不法所得追回。」下列何者是最可能完成此一要求的公務人員？

(A) 法官　　　(B) 法警　　　(C) 書記官　　　(D) 檢察官

12. 據報載，某雇主因擔心所雇用之勞工不聽指揮或中途離職，於是
扣留該受雇人之證件，約定在雇傭關係結束時就會同時歸還。對
於上述雇主的行為，下列敘述何者正確？

(A) 雇主可能已經觸法，該受雇者可尋求法律協助取回證件

(B) 雇主扣留證件雖具有強制性，但並不違背契約自由原則

(C) 雇主行為已侵害工作權，大法官會議可宣告此作法違憲

(D) 雇主扣留證件作為履行契約之保證，屬私法自治的範圍

13. 某甲因違反《集會遊行法》遭到檢察官起訴，法官在審理該案件時，認為該法部分條文有違憲疑慮，依據法律規定，下列何項作法較為妥適？
    (A) 法官可告知該案件之當事人，向司法院大法官提出釋憲聲請以解決此問題
    (B) 法官可暫停該訴訟審理，備齊理由向司法院大法官提出釋憲聲請以求解決
    (C) 該案件當事人可要求法官依惡法非法精神，認定該法條違憲並判決其無罪
    (D) 該案件當事人可根據信賴保護原則，對行政機關提出訴願要求撤銷原處分

14. 父母早逝、沒有妻小的獨子大德與年邁祖母相依為命。某日大德駕車不小心撞傷路人小芬，造成小芬身受重傷，約定賠償 50 萬元。一週後，大德因病身故，只留下存款 10 萬元，小芬只好轉向大德的祖母求償。關於上述賠償，下列選項何者正確？
    (A) 大德的祖母並非法律所定之繼承人，所以小芬的求償於法無據
    (B) 除非大德的祖母依法拋棄繼承，否則小芬可以向她求償 50 萬元
    (C) 就算大德的祖母未依法拋棄繼承，也只須對小芬負 10 萬元的清償責任
    (D) 肇事的人是大德，只有大德有賠償義務，小芬不可向大德的祖母求償

15. 表 2 為航空公司臺北飛航上海的方式、平均票價以及機位供給、需求狀況。請問以下描述或解釋不同飛行方式供需狀況差異的敘述何者正確？

表2

飛行方式	票價	機位供給	機位需求
臺北直飛上海	新臺幣 15,000 元	3,500 位	4,500 位
臺北經香港至上海	新臺幣 10,000 元	2,000 位	1,000 位

(A) 臺北直飛上海航班採以價制量導致需求大於供給

(B) 多數旅客並不認爲直飛的票價比轉機貴是合理的

(C) 只有少數航空公司有直飛上海，讓旅客無從選擇

(D) 數旅客認爲轉機額外的時間成本高於減價優惠

16. 因麵粉價格上漲影響大眾生活，政府要求麵粉業者必須將價格調回到漲價前的價格，且不得上漲。請問有關此凍漲措施的敘述何者正確？

(A) 雖會造成市場供不應求，但可提高經濟效率

(B) 會降低生產者剩餘，但消費者剩餘則會提高

(C) 此價格管制與政府保證收購農產品措施相同

(D) 會造成經濟效率的損失，非有必要不應施行

17. 部分非政府組織，爲提供經濟上弱勢的可可農較佳之貿易條件與更多機會，致力推廣公平貿易可可的販售。雖價格較高，但透過消費者多付一些錢，可幫助開發中國家可可農免於被剝削。此概念目前已漸爲民眾接受並積極參與，請問有關此現象的敘述何者正確？

(A) 顯示全球化貿易下利益分配失衡

(B) 此舉會讓可可農失去創新的動機

(C) 不符合絕對利益之資源配置原則

(D) 可可生產成本過高需要外界補貼

18. 國內生產毛額（GDP）、每人平均 GDP、綠色 GDP、國家競爭力以及經濟成長率等，皆爲衡量一國整體表現的指標。下列有關這些指標的敘述何者正確？
    (A) 一國的經濟成長率愈高，該國的 GDP 以及國家競爭力也愈高
    (B) GDP 無法顯示政府效能高低，但綠色 GDP 與國家競爭力則可
    (C) 經濟成長率較低國家之每人平均 GDP，不必然會低於經濟成長率較高國家
    (D) 相較於 GDP，綠色 GDP 因爲包含休閒價值，故後者的水準通常會高於前者

19. 當外部效果存在時，會破壞市場機能運作結果，進而影響資源分配以及經濟效率，請問有關外部效果影響的敘述何者正確？
    (A) 拍賣網站公布買賣雙方被評價內容，以克服因資訊不明產生的外部性問題
    (B) 高速公路以里程收費，乃依量出爲入原則提高政府收入，改善外部性問題
    (C) 以加油數量多寡收取空氣污染防制費，爲透過課稅方式解決外部成本問題
    (D) 書籍登記註冊爲透過確立財產權的方式，克服著作被盜印之政府失靈問題

20. 小明以悠遊卡搭乘捷運上班，到辦公室後享受公司免費供應的咖啡，下班後以折價券享用吃到飽晚餐。根據以上內容，請問下列敘述何者正確？
    (A) 若捷運車廂不擁擠，則雖有排他性但仍具共享性
    (B) 免費商品即是公共財，如小明辦公室供應的咖啡
    (C) 由於悠遊卡上未載明使用者姓名，故不算私有財
    (D) 使用折價券吃到飽之晚餐有共享性，沒有排他性

21-22 為題組

◎ 某學者研究指出：「1777 年廣東梅縣客家人羅芳伯在東南亞西婆羅洲，為抵抗盜匪與西方殖民者的入侵，遂帶領華人與當地原住民，採民族平等、融合共處的方式，成立『蘭芳大總制共和國』，進而建軍、頒布法令及徵收稅賦。其元首稱『大唐總長』，以選賢禪讓的形式傳承，而國之大事皆眾議而行。由於主其事者多為粵籍華人，基於民族情感的脈絡，仍向清朝納貢稱臣，……直到 19 世紀末，才被荷蘭人所滅……」。

21. 根據上述內容，下列對此一「國家」的敘述，何者較為正確？
　　(A) 他們向清朝納貢稱臣而無法自治，故仍是清朝版圖的一部分
　　(B) 因他們未加入國際聯盟組織，故其不是一個國際認可的國家
　　(C) 根據其政府的組成，應該是兼具總統制與內閣制特色的體制
　　(D) 其在所屬區域宣示主權並實施治權，應已具備國家組成要件

22. 前述蘭芳大總制共和國的描述，有關其「民主」的論述何者較為正確？
　　(A) 其採民族平等且大事皆眾議而行，基本展現民主共和精神
　　(B) 因其元首並非由人民選舉產生，欠缺代議民主的分權制衡
　　(C) 元首交替以禪讓方式傳承屬私相授受，不符依法行政原則
　　(D) 由於議會並無其他政黨成員，推論其政黨制度屬一黨優勢

23-24 為題組

◎ 民國 100 年臺灣社會爆發食物違法添加「塑化劑」的重大事件，引發各界重視。業者小華於民國 100 年 5 月因在食物中添加有害人體的「塑化劑」遭檢察官起訴。後因立法院認為原法律之處罰過輕，遂進行修法，對於違法者之處罰刑度由原來的三年以下有期徒刑，提高為七年以下有期徒刑，並自 100 年 6 月起生效。

23. 有食品業者發現其所使用的材料含有「塑化劑」，可能會危害食用者的健康，遂決定將產品從市面上全數回收。此一作法，主要是根據下列何者的要求？
(A) 《公平交易法》
(B) 《消費者保護法》
(C) 民法裡的過失責任原則
(D) 民法裡的公序良俗原則

24. 依上文內容，假設法院於同年 8 月就小華的行為判處其有期徒刑四年之刑罰，此判決之適法性為何？
(A) 合法，判決時新法已經生效，法官必須依據新修訂的法律審判
(B) 合法，法律本允許法官對於情節重大之犯罪酌量加重法定刑度
(C) 違法，因為在本案例法官應該依據行為人行為當時之法律審判
(D) 違法，此一判決未考慮社會觀感，不符合新法加重刑度的精神

25. 近代亞洲曾經爆發一場戰爭，交戰雙方都使用西方軍事技術及裝備。原本列強認為雙方旗鼓相當，但人口、土地均居下風的國家，因維新政策成功，反而戰勝，頗出各國意料。這場戰爭是：
(A) 日本打敗中國的甲午戰爭
(B) 以色列勝埃及的六日戰爭
(C) 越南擊敗美國的解放戰爭
(D) 印尼擊退荷蘭的獨立戰爭

26. 教科書往往反映當代的時局與世變。某一時期，小學課本中有一個單元名稱為「一個惡魔」，說「帝國主義是什麼？帝國主義是一個惡魔。他一隻手裡是算盤，一隻手裡是武器。他有兩副面孔，打算盤的時候，他的面孔好像很和善，但是，使用武器的時候，他的面孔就變得兇惡無比了。」還說：「他恐怕人家不如他的意，就想同人家訂不平等條約。」這應當是哪個時期的課本？

(A) 新文化運動時期   (B) 對日抗戰時期

(C) 文化大革命時期   (D) 臺灣戒嚴時期

27. 基督教會自「某個事件」開始，經常以宗教審判和贖罪券兩種方式強化教會的領導地位。宗教審判用以處罰危害教會的異端；贖罪券則用於酬謝參與打擊異教徒者，可免除死後審判。上述所說的「某個事件」是：

(A) 諾曼人入侵   (B) 十字軍運動

(C) 黑死病盛行   (D) 東羅馬滅亡

28. 一個展覽會中，主辦單位不僅邀請來自北海道、京都、大阪、朝鮮等地的機構與企業設館參展，也廣邀滿洲國、暹羅、福建等地的公私團體，展出各地特產。展場中另有一些具有特色的主題館，如糖業館與林業館。這是哪個展覽會的情況？

(A) 1935 年臺北的始政四十年博覽會

(B) 1970 年在大阪舉行的萬國博覽會

(C) 1975 年在沖繩的世界海洋博覽會

(D) 2010 年在上海舉行的世界博覽會

29. 1907 年，湖廣總督張之洞建議朝廷：禁止書鋪販售「某類物品」，違者重罰查封；並通令各省學堂，禁止學生購閱，違者逐出校門；令外務部商請總稅務司轉飭各郵政局，查禁銷毀，不得代寄。張之洞建議禁售的「某類物品」應是：

(A) 演論之書籍   (B) 基督教宣傳冊

(C) 憲政體制叢書   (D) 鼓吹革命書刊

30. 一本書的作者批評當時的社會現象，指出：世人喜歡利用祖先彰顯自己，例如王家已經遷居本地數代，但王某詩文集中卻仍標示百年前的祖籍，以證明家世顯赫。這本書最可能是：

(A) 漢代《風俗通義》　　　　　(B) 唐代《史通》

(C) 南宋《夷堅志》　　　　　　(D) 清代《皇朝通考》

31. 臺灣總督在就職時指出：「本政府統治方針本於『臺灣爲帝國領土之一部』的精神。我們應當啓發臺人之智能德操，使其感受朝廷一視同仁的美意，希望醇化臺人，使其與內地人融洽相處，進而使臺灣與內地無異。」這位總督最可能是：

(A) 1895 年接收臺灣，鎮壓抗日的樺山資紀

(B) 1902 年肅清「臺地匪亂」的兒玉源太郎

(C) 1919 年結束軍事統治的文官總督田健治郎

(D) 1936 年推動臺灣進入戰時體制的小林躋造

32. 一位政治人物呼籲：全國各黨各派要放棄歧見，停止內戰及一切敵對行爲；大家應當團結一致，抵禦外侮，集中力量來奮鬥救國。這種說法應是：

(A) 曾國藩對太平天國將領的招降公告

(B) 民國初年袁世凱稱帝時的登基宣言

(C) 九一八事變以後毛澤東的抗日聲明

(D) 抗戰勝利後蔣中正號召團結的主張

33. 一本書寫道：這個國家原本絕大多數人民爲農民，因社會發展不均，農民起而造反，爆發大革命，推翻既有政府，重建國家。新政府之施政目標是強化國防力量，以對抗資本主義國家，因此強調鋼鐵工業，民生工業的發展相對落後。但因該國實施計畫經濟，受到經濟恐慌的影響也較小。這最可能是描寫：

(A) 1790 年代的法國　　　　　(B) 1870 年代的日本

(C) 1930 年代的俄國　　　　　(D) 1970 年代的印度

34. 秦漢時期實施郡、縣二級的行政區劃,最基層的地方行政長官為
　　縣令(長),負責管理地方,統籌稅收。當時縣令(長)如何產
　　生?
　　(A) 根據宗法,父死子繼　　　　(B) 皇帝分封,册命任用
　　(C) 由郡守指派下屬擔任　　　　(D) 由中央政府直接任命

35. 1950 年代初期,歐洲某城市中,一位住在英國佔領區的居民,一
　　大早先通過檢哨站,到蘇聯佔領區上班。下班後,經常要繞到美
　　國佔領區購買日常用品,然後搭電車回家。這個人最可能生活在
　　何地?
　　(A) 維也納　　　　　　　　　　(B) 華沙
　　(C) 布拉格　　　　　　　　　　(D) 柏林

36. 一位學者擔心:國家因為民族多元,許多人受到當時流行的民族
　　主義影響,希望獨立、建國,最終可能導致國家分崩離析。他呼
　　籲大家珍惜共同擁有的歷史經驗,以「命運共同體」的觀念整合
　　國家。這位學者最可能生活在:
　　(A) 1860 年的義大利　　　　　　(B) 1910 年的奧匈帝國
　　(C) 1930 年的波蘭　　　　　　　(D) 1960 年的美國

37. 一位國家元首在議會中表示:統治者應當傾聽上帝的意旨,而不
　　受制於法律。他認為自己是人民的主人與父親,可以主宰臣民的
　　生死。他應當遵守與上帝的誓約,無須經過議會便可自行制訂法
　　律。這位元首是:
　　(A) 1 世紀羅馬統治者奧古斯都
　　(B) 17 世紀的英王詹姆士一世
　　(C) 19 世紀初法蘭西皇帝拿破崙
　　(D) 19 世紀末的德皇威廉二世

38. 一首讚美臺灣風情的歌謠說：「海岸線長山又高，處處港口都險要。四通八達有公路，南北是鐵道，太平洋上最前哨，臺灣稱寶島。」介紹物產時指出：「四季豐收蓬萊稻，農村多歡笑，白糖茶葉買賣好，家家戶戶吃得飽。鳳梨西瓜和香蕉，特產數不了，不管長住和初到，同聲齊誇耀。」這首歌謠創作的背景最可能是：
　(A) 1890 年代，臺灣慶祝第一條鐵路通車典禮
　(B) 1910 年代，日本總督府完成縱貫鐵路建設
　(C) 1950 年代，臺灣實施經濟改革，漸有成效
　(D) 1980 年代，中共統戰歌謠，爭取臺灣民心

39. 此一時期，君權高張，對於大臣、高官並不尊重。官員如觸怒天子，可能當眾遭到責罰，甚至押到午門外杖刑，年紀大的官員往往死於杖下。這本不是當時法典規範的刑罰，皇帝卻藉此樹立威望，壓抑大臣。這場景應發生於何時？
　(A) 漢朝　　　　　　　　　(B) 唐朝
　(C) 元朝　　　　　　　　　(D) 明朝

40. 一位統治者推動改革，規定：所有貴族、商人、軍人與城市居民都必須穿著日耳曼式服裝，違反法令者課以罰金。當時謠傳：我們的統治者其實是一位日耳曼理髮師冒充，所以要我們穿日耳曼式服裝。這些措施引起農民暴動，認為：我們捍衛基督信仰，卻因為穿著傳統服裝，不能進入教堂。這位統治者是：
　(A) 路易十四　　　　　　　(B) 彼得大帝
　(C) 明治天皇　　　　　　　(D) 凱末爾

41. 蔣中正在日記中記載：最近，中共代表向美國表示，中共必須重視莫斯科的意見，美國想調解國共關係，必須先徵求俄國同意。此段記載最可能出現於何時？

(A) 1924 年國民黨實施聯俄容共之際

(B) 1937 年七七盧溝橋事變爆發之後

(C) 1946 年二次大戰後中國發生內戰

(D) 1958 年中共發動八二三砲戰之前

42. 民國成立後,清史研究日漸盛行,對於清初「文字獄」提出了新的觀點與解釋。學者研究指出,部分民間傳聞與歷史事實之間有很大的差距。下列對此一現象的說明,何者最合理?

(A) 民間傳聞係來自革命黨人的醜化

(B) 學者受科學史觀影響,否定傳聞

(C) 清朝檔案偏袒皇帝,立場不客觀

(D) 宮中檔案開放,學者找到新事證

43. 表 3 爲 1910 年到 1940 年間臺灣人口的統計資料。

表3

年份	甲族群（萬）	比率%	乙族群（萬）	比率%	丙族群（萬）	比率%	丁族群（萬）	比率%	總計（萬）
1910	306	92.9	1.48	0.4	12.2	3.7	9.8	3.0	329.9
1920	343	91.4	2.48	0.7	13.0	3.5	16.6	4.4	375.7
1930	425	91.0	4.66	1.0	14.0	3.0	23.2	5.0	467.9
1940	552	90.9	4.61	0.8	15.8	2.6	34.6	5.7	607.7

表中丙、丁代表的族群分別是:

(A) 丙爲臺灣人、丁爲原住民

(B) 丙爲外國人、丁爲臺灣人

(C) 丙爲日本人、丁爲外國人

(D) 丙爲原住民、丁爲日本人

44. 某一政治活動中，許多民眾要求：政府必須保障非武裝之集會、結社的自由；政府應當保障言論、出版、罷工的自由；憲兵僅能管理軍人，不得隨意逮捕人犯；政府應當撤銷貿易局、專賣局。他們同時希望能保障生活必需品的供應。這是：
(A) 1789 年的法國革命
(B) 1830 年的七月革命
(C) 1947 年的二二八事件
(D) 1966 年的文化大革命

45. 某一地區在 15 世紀初逐漸成為國際貿易中心，各地商人在此交易，也可乘船前往中國經商。當地國王與中國建立友好關係，曾親自前往北京，中國使臣也經常前往該地。16 世紀，該地遭西方殖民者入侵，國際貿易形勢改變，東西文明往來更為頻繁。這個地區是：
(A) 麻六甲
(B) 臺灣
(C) 琉球
(D) 香港

46. 一座城市中，居民熱烈討論即將重建的大教堂建築樣式，他們對常見的哥德式建築並不滿意。因為古代建築廢墟隨處可見，他們鼓勵競標的建築師從古代建築中尋找靈感。經過幾十年的努力，一座覆以圓頂的長方形教堂，終告竣工。這座城市是：
(A) 羅馬帝國時期的耶路撒冷
(B) 十一世紀中期的聖彼得堡
(C) 文藝復興時期的佛羅倫斯
(D) 十九世紀初期的墨西哥市

47-48 為題組

◎ 新航路暢通之後，國際人口移動逐漸增加，許多地區成了移民的目標。18 世紀以後，出現許多移民組成的新國家。

47. 一個由歐洲移民主導的國家，立法者將國內人口分成「白人」與「非白人」兩類。20 世紀初年，該國政府計畫制訂移民政策時，打算將所有申請移民該國的人口分成「可以」與「不可」被白人社會同化兩類。他們認定非白人屬「次等種族」，會降低該國生活品質，必須防止非白人破壞既有的美好生活。這個國家是：
    - (A) 澳洲
    - (B) 美國
    - (C) 俄國
    - (D) 新加坡

48. 這種想法應是受到何種思想影響？
    - (A) 社會達爾文主義
    - (B) 馬克思共產主義
    - (C) 啟蒙運動思潮
    - (D) 理性主義思潮

49. 照片 1 是某人站在樹林裡的小徑，由南向北拍攝的某地地表景觀。從照片中可判斷該地正在發生何種變化？
    - (A) 斷層作用由南向北不斷延伸
    - (B) 背斜構造由東向西逐漸隆起
    - (C) 堆積作用由北向南陸續增強
    - (D) 坡地地層由西向東緩慢滑動

照片 1

50. 長期以來，印尼即以「關係印尼民族生死存亡的問題」為由，推動「國內移民」計畫。從 1960 年代到 1980 年代，共有 100 萬左右的家庭遷移他處。下列哪兩個因素是印尼推行國內移民計畫的主因？（甲）促進區域開發（乙）爪哇島居民過多（丙）土地分配不均（丁）民族混居動亂頻繁。
    - (A) 甲乙
    - (B) 甲丁
    - (C) 乙丙
    - (D) 丙丁

51. 圖 1 是某地等高線地形圖，圖中甲、乙、丙、丁為養豬戶所在，
X 線段是預計要修築水壩的位置。
若水壩修築完成，則哪家養豬戶必
須遷移，以免污染水庫水源？

(A) 甲
(B) 乙
(C) 丙
(D) 丁

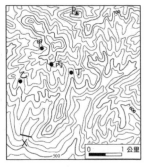

圖 1

52. 重大政治或經濟事件發生時，常立即影響全球股票價格。若上海
在當地凌晨 2 時 30 分發生足以影響全球股市的重大事件，則香港
（營業時間：9:30-16:00）、倫敦（營業時間：8:00-16:00）、紐
約（營業時間：8:30-15:00）、東京（營業時間：9:00-15:00）等
地的股票市場，發生股價波動的先後順序為何？

(A) 紐約、倫敦、香港、東京　　(B) 倫敦、香港、東京、紐約
(C) 香港、倫敦、紐約、東京　　(D) 紐約、東京、香港、倫敦

53. 聯合國教科文組織登錄的世界遺產，包括自然遺產、文化遺產和
複合遺產三大類。日本登錄的世界遺產中，有 12 項屬文化遺產。
從日本的歷史發展判斷，圖 2 中何處擁有的文化遺產最多？

(A) 甲
(B) 乙
(C) 丙
(D) 丁

圖 2

54. 英國風險顧問公司指出，全球對天災最無招架之力的第一名國家
    是孟加拉，面臨「極度」風險的第一名國家也是孟加拉。孟加拉
    面臨的天災經常發生在每年的哪一季節？
    (A) 春季　　　　(B) 夏季　　　　(C) 秋季　　　　(D) 冬季

55. 圖3為某高科技產品製造公司 I-IV 四個不同時期的區位變遷圖。
    下列哪個概念最適合解釋這種變遷？
    (A) 區位租
    (B) 區位擴散
    (C) 區位慣性
    (D) 位聚集

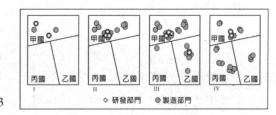

圖3

56. 2012年聯合國糧食暨農業組織（FAO）表示：「糧食不足和營養
    不良再度席捲該區，約1800萬人直接受害。乾旱使得該區的穀物
    生產較去年減少26%，當地的游牧因嚴重的飼料短缺而提早移動，
    移動路線也因此改變，導致邊界地帶的緊張升高。」引文裡的「該
    區」最可能位於圖4中哪個位置？
    (A) 甲
    (B) 乙
    (C) 丙
    (D) 丁

圖4

57. 透過地圖的比對，常可用來探究地形變遷或土地利用變化的過程。
    臺灣在過去一百餘年來，曾陸續出版過數套比例尺為 1:20000 或
    1:25000 的等高線地形圖。下列哪些研究課題，其變遷過程可經由

這些地圖的比對來進行？（甲）彰雲地區濁水溪河道變遷（乙）宜蘭縣海岸的沙丘縮減（丙）苗栗大安溪河川地農地增加（丁）屏東墾丁洋蔥栽培面積的變化。

(A) 甲乙丙　　　(B) 甲乙丁　　　(C) 甲丙丁　　　(D) 乙丙丁

58-59 為題組

◎ 以全球的尺度而言，活動沙丘主要分布在海岸地帶、乾燥地區和冰河區的外緣。請問：

58. 海岸地帶、乾燥地區和冰河區外緣，活動沙丘容易發育的主要原因為何？
    (A) 風向變化少
    (B) 植被覆蓋稀
    (C) 地表高度低
    (D) 年降水量微

59. 乾燥地區的沙丘，組成物質疏鬆，當其化育成為砂土時，此種砂土具有下列哪項特徵？
    (A) 土壤質地均勻，土層透水性良好
    (B) O層發育明顯，有機質含量豐富
    (C) 土壤化育成熟度較高，層次分明
    (D) 淋溶作用旺盛，土壤多為酸性土

60-61 為題組

◎ 圖 5 為某地區某一農場的工作年曆。請問：

60. 該農場最可能出現於下列何地？
    (A) 歐洲西北部
    (B) 非洲西南部
    (C) 北美東北部
    (D) 澳洲東南部

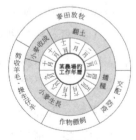

圖 5

61. 圖 6 是美國農業分區圖。圖 5 所代表的農業類型，在圖 6 甲、乙、
    丙、丁四地區中，何區的分布最普遍？

    (A) 甲
    (B) 乙
    (C) 丙
    (D) 丁

圖 6

62-63 為題組

◎ 近年來，有些地理學家從均衡區域發展和區域合作的角度，研議
  將中國的三大經濟地帶調整。建議調整後的新三大地帶為：

東北及東部區（黑龍江、
吉林、遼寧、河北、北
京、天津、山東、江蘇、
上海、浙江、福建、廣
東、海南）；中部及近
西部區（山西、陝西、
寧夏、甘肅、河南、安
徽、江西、湖北、湖南、
重慶、四川、廣西、貴
州、雲南）和遠西部區
（內蒙古、新疆、青海、
西藏）。

表 4

區域代號 產業部門	三大經濟地帶 （1985 年畫分）		
	甲	乙	丙
第一級產業	46.67	28.34	40.58
第二級產業	19.66	35.02	26.19
第三級產業	33.68	36.64	33.23

區域代號 產業部門	新三大地帶 （近年研議）		
	丁	戊	己
第一級產業	43.94	48.82	27.52
第二級產業	24.06	16.43	34.93
第三級產業	32.00	34.75	37.56

表 4 是三大經濟地帶和調整後新三大地帶各區三級產業就業人口
比例資料，請問：

62. 近年來，中國工業用水和都市民生用水缺水問題最嚴重的地區，分別出現在「三大經濟地帶」和「新三大地帶」的何處？
(A) 甲、丁
(B) 甲、戊
(C) 乙、己
(D) 丙、丁

63. 中國水資源分布不均，近年來，有些地區缺水問題日益嚴重，南水北調計畫應運而生。南水北調計畫的「中線」，調水路線分別跨越「三大經濟地帶」和「新三大地帶」的哪兩區？
(A) 甲乙、戊己
(B) 甲丙、戊己
(C) 乙丙、丁戊
(D) 乙丙、丁己

64-66 為題組

◎ 某同學在環島旅行的過程中，曾搭乘照片 2 所示的四路公車。各車的行車標示分別是：甲車：恆春—鵬園；乙車：南寮—竹科；丙車：台中—水里；丁車：花蓮火車站—梨山。請問：

64. 該同學前往探究清代牡丹社事件發生的地理背景時，搭乘的是哪輛公車？
(A) 甲
(B) 乙
(C) 丙
(D) 丁

65. 哪個縣市的轄境，會有圖中的兩路公車行駛？
(A) 屏東縣
(B) 花蓮縣
(C) 南投縣
(D) 台中市

照片 2

66. 如果該同學從雲林縣出發，以順時針方向進行環島旅行，旅行途中曾先後搭乘過這四輛公車。該同學搭乘這四輛公車的先後順序是：
    (A) 甲乙丁丙
    (B) 甲丙丁乙
    (C) 乙甲丙丁
    (D) 丙乙丁甲

67-69 為題組

◎ 2011 年，聯合國世界觀光旅遊組織（UNWTO）公布，世界觀光旅遊競爭力和國外旅客到訪人數前十名的國家，如表 5 所示。請問：

表 5

觀光旅遊競爭力			國外旅客到訪人數		
國家	世界排名	競爭力指數	國家	世界排名	（百萬人）
瑞士	1	5.68	法國	1	76.80
德國	2	5.50	美國	2	59.75
法國	3	5.41	中國	3	55.67
奧地利	4	5.41	西班牙	4	52.68
瑞典	5	5.34	義大利	5	43.63
美國	6	5.30	英國	6	28.13
英國	7	5.30	土耳其	7	27.00
西班牙	8	5.29	德國	8	26.88
加拿大	9	5.29	馬來西亞	9	24.58
新加坡	10	5.23	墨西哥	10	22.40

67. 在觀光旅遊競爭力最強的十國中，最多國家皆有的自然觀光資源為何？
    (A) 冰河地形
    (B) 熔岩台地
    (C) 石林岩漠
    (D) 環礁潟湖

68. 在國外旅客到訪人數最多的前十國中，哪個海域周邊的國家，吸引的國外旅客人數最多？
    (A) 南海　　　　(B) 北海　　　　(C) 地中海　　　(D) 加勒比海

69. 根據表 5 的資料，下列哪項推論最為合理？
    (A) 觀光遊憩產業的發達程度，和人類發展程度指標的高低呈正相關
    (B) 觀光遊憩資源的數量多寡，和陸地與水域面積比例大小呈負相關
    (C) 觀光遊憩產業的區位選擇，和居民宗教信仰的多元程度呈正相關
    (D) 觀光遊憩產業商圈的規模，和國家歷史文化的時間長短呈負相關

70-72 為題組

◎ 圖 7 是經過處理的福爾摩沙二號衛星影像，圖 8 是從衛星影像中某地針對耕地方向的素描圖。請問：

70. 圖 7 中河流主流兩側的山地，分別屬於哪兩座山脈？
    (A) 海岸山脈、中央山脈　　　(B) 中央山脈、雪山山脈
    (C) 雪山山脈、玉山山脈　　　(D) 玉山山脈、阿里山山脈

71. 圖 8 是從圖 7 中哪個地點向哪個方向所畫的素描？
    (A) 甲，南南西　　　　(B) 乙，南南東
    (C) 丙，北北東　　　　(D) 丁，北北西

72. 目前圖7、圖8中「耕地」最可能出現的作物為何？
    (A)咖啡　　　　(B) 菸草　　　　(C) 鳳梨　　　　(D) 蔬菜

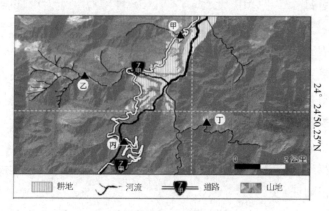

圖 7

圖 8

102年度學科能力測驗社會科試題詳解

單選題

1. **D**

【解析】『改善對異文化所產生的刻板印象』，唯有透過相互的交流與互動，才能有效的增進彼此的瞭解，破除『刻板印象』，而 (A) (B) (C) 相對與 (D) 各大學辦理學生交換，其交流層面都較少。

2. **C**

【解析】依據天賦人權的觀點，生而為人即享有人權，因此 (C) 觀光客非我國國民當然不具有『公民權』(如選舉、罷免等)，但仍享有『人權』。

3. **A**

【解析】(A) 在新聞自由的環境下，各媒體會因其各自的背景、歷史，甚至經營者的理念等因素，各有不同的新聞立場，因此對同一新聞事件各家媒體解讀不同或報導迥異，應為常態。

(B) 媒體若為擴大自家報社的市場占有率 ，可能會迎合大眾意見或觀點，但此處無法說明為何兩者『報導迥異』。

4. **B**

【解析】『倡議，指公民可以透過意見表達來形成輿論，以影響政府施政。』，而題目所詢問的是『公民團體的倡議』，因此 (B) 有志人士組成妓權團體 (屬公民團體)，遊說政府…，較為適合。

5. **C**

【解析】 主我，爲『主觀、未社會化、易衝動、具創造力的我』；
客我，爲『客觀、已社會化、遵守規範的我』，因此

(A) 接受社會規範，應爲客我，

(B) 主我較容易表現出衝動

(C) 因主我較具創造力，所以受主我影響的自我也會較
具創造力

(D) 個人自我成長的過程中，存在著主我與客我的互動
與衝突，因此不只是『和諧互動』。

6. **D**

【解析】 志願結社指由人民自發由下而上地組織起來，爲實現特
定目標而組織形成的團體。

(A) 政黨也屬志願結社

(B) 志願結社並不一定要向政府正式立案登記

(C) 志願結社，並不必然與政府對抗

(D) 志願結社仍可進行營利行爲（如企業性經營或活
動），但不會進行分紅，而是將營利所得作爲社團的
營運經費。

7. **C**

【解析】 (A) 總統選舉採相對多數制，因此只有一輪投票

(B) 市長選舉，仍採單一選區『相對』多數決制

(D) 立法委員選舉採單一選區兩票制。

8. **B**

【解析】 政策合法化指『將決定之方案，送交有關單位加以審議
核准，完成立法程序，通常由民意機關通過』。因此 (B)
較爲正確（經縣議會表決通過）。

9. **C**

【解析】　蔣經國總統的『三不政策：不接觸、不談判、不妥協』、
陳水扁總統的「四不：不宣佈獨立、不更改國號、不推
動兩國論入憲、不推動改變現狀的統獨公投；一沒有：
沒有廢除國統綱領與國統會的問題」、馬英九總統「新
三不：不統、不獨、不武」，因此

(A) 「三不」政策時期，兩岸關係仍然以不接觸為原則

(B) 「四不」中的『不推動兩國論入憲』，即表示並不
『堅持一邊一國』的主張

(D) 「四不」與「三不」兩者在立場上差異甚大。

10. **B**

【解析】　依表一該國國會總席次為100席，因此本次選舉並無政
黨取得過半席次，

(A) 甲黨席次雖少，但其他政黨在籌組聯合內閣時，仍
可能會與該黨合作

(B) 丙黨若想籌組聯合內閣，可能出現『甲乙丙』、『乙
丙丁』等組合方式，會與多個政黨分享內閣權力，
而若與戊黨合作，則只需與一個政黨分享權力。

(C) 甲乙丁三黨組成聯合內閣，並未過半

(D) 乙丙兩黨若合作組閣，就有47席，因此與甲黨、丁
黨或戊黨合作皆可過半。

11. **D**

【解析】　檢察官對於犯罪等違法情事，依法應主動偵查、追訴犯
罪，並依證據向法院起訴。

12. **A**

【解析】　(A) (B) 依據就業服務法第54條：『雇主聘僱外國人不得
有下列情事：八、非法扣留或侵占所聘僱外國人之

護照、居留證件或財物。』，個人證件屬私人物品，
依法不得任意扣留，因此不適用契約自由。

(C) 扣留證件並未侵害工作權，且依據不告不理原則，
大法官會議不能主動釋憲。

(D) 私法自治不得違反法律強制或禁止規定，而『雇主
扣留證件』爲法律所禁止的行爲。

13. **B**

【解析】 (B) 各級法院法官於審理案件時，對於適用之法律認爲
有違憲之疑義者，得先停止訴訟，聲請大法官解釋。

14. **C**

【解析】 (A) (D) 繼承順位爲：直系血親卑親屬→父母→兄弟姊妹
→祖父母，因大德『父母早逝、沒有妻小且爲獨子』，
因此祖母爲其第四順位繼承人 (B) (C) 我國目前之繼承制
度爲『全面限定繼承』(繼承人只從繼承財產來償還被
繼承人之債務)，且大德只留下存款 10 萬元，因此祖母
只須對小芬負 10 萬元的清償責任。

15. **D**

【解析】 (A) 依題意臺北直飛上海航班，需求大於供給，因此表
示直飛的票價低於市場價格，而『以價制量』則是
指藉由提高價格來抑制需求量，而由題目中並無此
現象。

(B) 直飛的需求大於供給，因此表示多數旅客應認爲直
飛的票價是合理的

(C) 直飛的機位較轉機爲多，因此直飛上海的航空公司
應該較轉機爲多。

16. **D**

　　【解析】　『政府要求麵粉業者必須將價格調回到漲價前的價格，
　　　　　　　且不得上漲。』表示，政府進行價格管制，制訂『價格
　　　　　　　上限』，規定售價必須低於市場價格，因此

　　　　　　(A) (D) 售價下降，會降低供給者供給意願，造成市場供
　　　　　　　　　 不應求，但依經濟學概念政府管制會產生無謂損失，
　　　　　　　　　 因此會降低經濟效率

　　　　　　(B) 因價格下降，會降低生產者剩餘，因為會產生無謂損
　　　　　　　　 失，所以消費者剩餘不一定會提高

　　　　　　(C) 政府保證收購農產品，是指政府以高於市場價格來收
　　　　　　　　 購農產，為『價格下限』。

17. **A**

　　【解析】　(A) 在全球化下所標榜的自由貿易，引發一些弊病，如
　　　　　　　　　 貧富差距擴大、經濟強勢國家對於弱勢國家剝削⋯
　　　　　　　　　 等問題，使得國際間開始提倡『公平貿易』。

18. **C**

　　【解析】　(A) 一國的經濟成長率愈高，表示今年的 GDP，相對於
　　　　　　　　　 去年的 GDP 高出許多，差距越大經濟成長率越高，
　　　　　　　　　 但不表示『該國的 GDP 越高』；而國家競爭力是一
　　　　　　　　　 項綜合判斷，考量因素包含政府效能等，因此不能
　　　　　　　　　 單就『經濟成長率』來判斷該國的國家競爭力

　　　　　　(B) 綠色 GDP 著重於衡量經濟發展對於生態、環境的影
　　　　　　　　 響，並無考量『政府效能』；而國家競爭力則是『政
　　　　　　　　 府效能』的內涵之一

　　　　　　(C) 每人平均 GDP 是以 GDP/人口數，因各國人口數不
　　　　　　　　 同，故經濟成長率較低國家之每人平均 GDP，不必
　　　　　　　　 然會低於經濟成長率較高國家

(D) 綠色 GDP = GDP－折舊－自然資源消耗及環境品
質變化，並未包含休閒價值，因此綠色 GDP 之數據
會低於 GDP。

19. **A 或 C**

【解析】 (B) 高速公路以里程收費，屬『使用者付費』的精神，避
免資源濫用的（公共財）外部性問題

(D) 政府失靈指政府為解決市場失靈，而採行各種政策，
但政策無法充分發揮作用，甚至引發更大的問題。
書籍登記註冊可達到確立財產權的效果，且並非政
府作為，因此非政府失靈，應改為有助於克服被盜
印之市場失靈問題。

20. **A**

【解析】 私有財與公共財的分類

性質	無法排他性	可排他性
共享性	公共財（純公共財） 國防、治安 （不擁擠又不收費的道路）	準公共財 高速公路、有線電視 （不擁擠但收費的道路）
獨享性	準私有財 野生動物、公海生物 （擁擠但不收費的道路）	純私有財(私有財)， 私人財產、住宅 （擁擠又收費的道路）

(A) 捷運車廂不擁擠：共享性、可排他性

(B) 公共財為共享及不可有排他性，因此辦公室免費咖
啡，具有不可排他性，但並非無限量因此不具共享
性

(C) 悠遊卡雖未載明使用者姓名，但一次只能供一人使用，且使用後會扣除款項，因此屬私有財

(D) 吃到飽原則上會無限量供應，因此具有共享性，但並非免費因此有排他性。

21-22 為題組

21. **D**

【解析】 (A)(D) 國家的組成要素為『人民、領土、政府、主權』，依題意『蘭芳大總制共和國』已具有國家性質，『人民（帶領華人與當地原住民）、領土（東南亞西婆羅洲）、政府、主權（建軍、頒布法令及徵收稅賦，並產生元首『大唐總長』)』，非清朝的一部分

(B) 加入國際聯盟組織，並非國家的必要條件

(C) 無法判斷。

22. **A**

【解析】 (B) 依題意『元首以選賢禪讓的形式傳承，而國之大事皆眾議而行』，因此元首雖非人民選舉產生，但國民可參與政策之制訂與討論，故仍有制衡機制，元首並非獨裁

(C) 若『元首禪讓方式』為國民的共識，並依此共識執行，就符合依法行政原則

(D) 題目中並未提及議會制度及政黨制度，故無法判斷。

23-24 為題組

23. **B**

【解析】 消費者保護法，之立法目的為防止企業經營者以不正當的手段來獲取利益，對民眾權益造成侵害，因此依題意『食品業者發現…含有「塑化劑」…遂決定將產品回收』，此即消保法對企業經營者所課之責任。

24. **C**

   【解析】 依據『不溯及既往原則』，立法院後來修訂之新法（…提高爲七年以下有期徒刑…），除非有例外，否則只能適用法律通過後所爲之行爲，因此就本案只能適用『行爲時之法律』（…原來的三年以下有期徒刑…）。

25. **A**

   【解析】(A) 此題關鍵處在「人口、土地均居下風的國家，因維新政策成功，反而戰勝」，因甲午戰前日本人口、土地均居下風；中國和日本海軍軍力，據唐德剛所述「當年大清帝國海上武裝，居世界海軍第八位；在甲午前夕，日本海軍全部噸位砲位及海戰潛力，實遠落中國之後，在世界排名僅爲第十六位」，中國「自強運動」船堅　利未成功，反而日本「明治維新」舉國上下努力，故打敗中國，頗出各國意料。

26. **A**

   【解析】(A) 新文化運動影響五四運動，五四運動是學生救亡圖存的愛國運動，促成社會各階層普遍的覺醒，加深國人尋求國家自立圖強的意識，並擴大新文化運動的影響，影響日後反軍閥、反列強的風潮，故題幹中有「帝國主義是一個惡魔……，一隻手裡是武器……使用武器的時候，他的面孔就變得兇惡無比了。」；其他答案時期沒有反帝國主義浪潮。

27. **B**

   【解析】(B) 由題幹中「打擊異教徒者」可知是「十字軍運動」；『贖罪券』（Indulgence）（赦罪券、赦罪符），其正式名稱爲大赦；售賣『贖罪券』源於十一世紀「十字軍時代」，1095年教宗烏爾班二世（Urban II）規定：凡

冒生命危險參與保衛耶路撒冷教會（不爲求取自身的光榮）的十字軍「聖戰」信徒可獲得『贖罪券』，可以抵銷所有的罪罰（暫罰）──大赦只能寬赦暫罰，並不能赦罪。

28. **A**

【解析】　(A) 此題關鍵處在「滿洲國」，滿洲國成立時間 1932-45 年，故選 (A) 1935年臺北的始政四十年博覽會；1935 年臺灣總督府爲宣揚治臺政績，在臺北舉行「始政四十週年紀念臺灣博覽會」，分別以臺北市公會堂（現在的中山堂）、臺北市公園（現在的二二八公園）、大稻埕分場與草山溫泉池（現在的陽明山溫泉）四大展示區，讓海內外人士了解總督府在臺灣的經營成果，其他答案時間不對。

29. **D**

【解析】　(D) 1907年（清末）張之洞建議禁售的「某類物品」應是鼓吹革命書刊，因爲當時革命風潮正興，清廷極力打壓革命，故禁「鼓吹革命書刊」；

　　　　　(A) 『天演論』是嚴復翻譯鼓吹維新運動（戊戌變法）的著作，八國聯軍後慈禧太后推動庚子後新政（慈禧變法），內容與戊戌變法類似，不可能禁；

　　　　　(B) 英法聯軍天津條約後基督教士可自由在中國各地遊歷傳教，不可能禁「基督教宣傳冊」；

　　　　　(C) 1905日俄戰後，中國推動「立憲運動」，「憲政體制叢書」不可能禁。

30. **B**

【解析】　(B) 唐代黃巢之亂前，中國仍重視家族門第，故「世人喜歡利用祖先彰顯自己，例如王家已經遷居本地數代，

但王某詩文集中卻仍標示百年前的祖籍,以證明家世
顯赫」,唐代劉知幾《史通》中批評當時這種社會現
象;其他答案時期不重視家族門第。

31. **C**

【解析】 (C) 此題關鍵處在「希望醇化臺人,使其與內地人融洽相
處,進而使臺灣與內地無異」,1919年一次世界大戰
後美國總統威爾遜的「民族自決」主張流行,田健治
郎首任文官總督在台灣推動「日臺一體」同化政策
(內地延長主義),台灣逐漸同化為日本領土。

32. **C**

【解析】 (C) 此題關鍵處在「全國各黨各派要放棄歧見,停止內戰
及一切敵對行為;大家應當團結一致,抵禦外侮」,
可知為 (C) 九一八事變以後毛澤東的抗日聲明;因民
國初年中國軍閥割據南北混戰(1917-1928年)、國共
對抗,北伐後又爆發中原大戰(1929-30年),此時日
本等侵略中國日亟,故號召全國各黨各派應當團結一
致,抵禦外侮。

33. **C**

【解析】 (C) 1917年列寧等領導布爾什維克(Bolshevik,後來的
俄國共產黨)發動攻擊奪取政權,史稱「十月革命」,
建立蘇聯政權,後列寧改行「新經濟政策」(New
Economic Policy,NEP),俄國經濟逐步復甦;史達
林開始實施「五年計畫」,五年經濟計畫壯大蘇聯的
工業,卻犧牲民生經濟,受到經濟恐慌的影響也較
小,讓人以為蘇聯式的計畫經濟有可取之處,導致社
會主義勢力抬頭。

34. **D**

【解析】 (D) 從春秋楚國、晉國等併吞土地後，不封子孫而置
　　　　　　「郡」「縣」，最基層的地方長官為縣令（長），
　　　　　　負責管理地方，統籌稅收。當時縣令（長）由中央政
　　　　　　府直接任命，治理地方；錢穆指東周「內廢公族（廢
　　　　　　封建），外務兼併（行郡縣）」，秦漢時期沿襲。

35. **D 或 A**

【解析】 (D) 第二次世界大戰後，蘇聯占領東柏林，美、英、法占
　　　　　　領西柏林；西柏林在東德境內，成為自由的孤島；蘇
　　　　　　聯為報復西方民主國家與它作對，在 1948 年 6 月開
　　　　　　始封鎖西柏林，企圖壓迫美、英、法退出西柏林；西方
　　　　　　三國利用空運方式運送民生物品接濟西柏林的軍民。

36. **B**

【解析】 (B) 1867年建立的奧匈（Austria-Hungary）帝國是匈牙利
　　　　　　貴族與奧地利哈布斯堡王朝在爭取維持原來的奧地利
　　　　　　帝國時達成的折衷方案，1910 年的奧匈帝國是一個多
　　　　　　民族國家，11 個主要民族（日耳曼人、匈牙利人、
　　　　　　捷克人、波蘭人、烏克蘭人、斯洛維尼亞人、義大利
　　　　　　人、羅馬尼亞人、斯洛伐克人、克羅埃西亞人和塞爾
　　　　　　維亞人），許多人受到當時流行的民族主義影響，希
　　　　　　望獨立建國，當時奧皇弗朗茲．約瑟夫一世（Franz
　　　　　　Josef I，1830年－1916年）呼籲大家珍惜共同擁有的
　　　　　　歷史經驗，以「命運共同體」的觀念整合國家；其他
　　　　　　答案的國家民族不多元。

37. **B**

【解析】 (B) 此題關鍵處在「統治者應當傾聽上帝的意旨，而不受
　　　　　　制於法律……他應當遵守與上帝的誓約，無須經過議

會便可自行制訂法律」，此即「君權神授」說，歐洲
的專制政治在十七、八世紀發展到高峰，各國君主強
調「君權神授」，代表人物是法王路易十四（Louis
XIV,1643－1715年）、英王詹姆士一世（James I，
1566－1625年）。

38. **C**

【解析】 (C) 此題關鍵處在「不管長住和初到，同聲齊誇耀」，「長
住」指本省人，「初到」指外省人，故選 (C) 1950 年
代，臺灣實施經濟改革，漸有成效；

(A) 「南北是鐵道」－台灣縱貫鐵路完成於 1908 年，與
答案（1890年代）不符合；

(B) 「四季豐收蓬萊稻」於1926年成功栽培，與答案
（1910年代）不符合。

39. **D**

【解析】 (D) 明太祖朱元璋時，君權高張，常以「廷杖」（朝臣有
過失，在殿廷上杖打朝臣，嚴重傷害文人的尊嚴）
和「文字獄」（因文字使用不當而殺人或抓人坐牢）
羞辱文人。

40. **B**

【解析】 (B) 彼得大帝（Peter the Great，1682－1725）積極西化，
施行富國強兵之策，才使古老的俄國擺脫中世紀的封
閉與落後；他下令剪除長袍肥大的袖管，改以日耳曼
式的服裝作為俄人服飾；此外彼得大帝下令禁止蓄
鬍，然而蓄鬍是俄國東正教徒的古老習慣，蓄鬍代表
人格的完整，剃鬍是違反基督教教義的行為，彼得大
帝改採折衷辦法，改納鬍鬚稅。

41. **C**

【解析】 (C) 二次世界大戰後中國發生國共內戰時,美國先派赫爾利(Hurley)於民國 33 年來華調停國共紛爭,促成重慶會談召開;後派馬歇爾(Marshall)1945-47 年來華,促成國共停戰協定,並召開政治協商會議;故中共代表向美國表示,中共必須重視莫斯科的意見,美國想調解國共關係,必須先徵求俄國同意。

42. **D**

【解析】 (D) 宮中檔案開放,學者找到新事證,清初「文字獄」提出了新的觀點與解釋;如呂留良歷經百餘年官方強加之記憶,悖逆的形象確立,直至清末民初,呂留良重新接受另一波轉化;從種種的資料呈現,呂留良無反清的意圖或行動。

43. **D**

【解析】 (D) 此題關鍵處在丁族群,由教材可知日治時期在臺日人人數不多,1943 年時約四十萬人,僅占當時總人口六百多萬人的百分之六,可知丁為日本人;甲:台灣人、乙:外國人、丙:原住民。

44. **C**

【解析】 (C) 此題關鍵處在「政府應當撤銷貿易局、專賣局」,因 1947 年的二二八事件政府接收日產變為公營事業,推行專賣制度,扼殺商機,又因捲入國共內戰,米、糖等物資被大量輸往中國,物價飛漲,故當時代表要求撤銷貿易局、專賣局,同時希望能保障生活必需品的供應;二二八事件後政府縮小公營事業範圍,擴大私人經濟活動空間,將專賣局改制為菸酒公賣局,開放樟腦、火柴業民營,允許民營煤礦;其他答案無此現象。

45. **A**

　　【解析】(A) 十五、十六世紀西方大航海時代出現，歐洲人在東南
　　　　　　　　亞建立殖民統治，這些歐洲殖民政府知道和中國進行
　　　　　　　　貿易帶來的大利益，非常重視華商，麻六甲先後為葡
　　　　　　　　萄牙、荷蘭與英國佔領統治，逐漸成為國際貿易中心，
　　　　　　　　東西文明往來更為頻繁；其他答案的地區無此現象。

46. **C**

　　【解析】(C) 中古時期歐洲建築出現哥德式和羅馬式風格，題幹中
　　　　　　　　「居民熱烈討論即將重建的大教堂建築樣式，他們對
　　　　　　　　常見的哥德式建築並不滿意。因為古代建築廢墟隨處
　　　　　　　　可見，他們鼓勵競標的建築師從古代建築中尋找靈
　　　　　　　　感」，可知為古希臘、羅馬文化再生的文藝復興時期
　　　　　　　　的佛羅倫斯。

47-48 為題組

47. **A**

　　【解析】(A) 由題幹「歐洲移民主導的國家」可知此為澳洲或美
　　　　　　　　國，二十世紀初，該國政府計畫制訂移民政策時，將
　　　　　　　　非白人定義為「次等種族」，會降低該國生活品質，
　　　　　　　　必須防止非白人破壞既有的美好生活，可知是澳洲的
　　　　　　　　「白澳政策」（White Australia Policy）。

48. **A**

　　【解析】(A) 此題題幹『認定非白人屬「次等種族」』，可知為「白
　　　　　　　　種人優越論」，應是「社會達爾文主義」（Social
　　　　　　　　Darwinism）的影響，這種理論被濫用，成為帝國主
　　　　　　　　義向外侵略的理論基礎。

49. **D**

【解析】 1. 因照片是在小徑由南向北拍攝，故判知照片方位為：
北上南下、右東左西。

2. 照片中樹幹根部彎曲，為地層發生崩壞作用「潛移」
的證據；由樹幹基部向東彎曲，証明坡地地層長時間
緩慢由西→東滑動。

50. **A**

【解析】 1. 印尼人口壓力沉重（2.4億人、2010年）：青壯人口約
占 2/3，雖供應充沛勞力，但失業率高、貧窮人口多。

2. 人口分布不均：印尼人口密度雖僅 128人/平方公里，
但六成以上人口集中面積僅占 7% 的爪哇島，人口過
於集中，地狹人稠，造成嚴重環境壓力；而「外島」
邊陲區人口稀疏。故實施國內移民計畫，將爪哇人口
移向蘇門答臘、加里曼丹、蘇拉威西等人口較少的島
嶼，有助於區域開發。

51. **C**

【解析】 由等高線地形圖判讀 (丙) 位X水壩上游集水區，最可能
污染水庫水源。

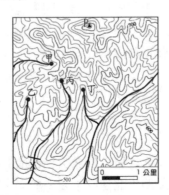

52. **D**

【解析】 由四地時區位置可判斷股價波動順序：紐約→東京→香港→倫敦。

53. **C**

【解析】 丙區域內的京都、奈良是日本古都，具有豐富的歷史古蹟與文化遺產。

54. **B**

【解析】 孟加拉的天災與夏季季風及夏季熱帶氣旋相關，多發生在夏季。

1. 孟加拉的水、旱災：主要源於夏季西南季風進退的時間太早或太晚，及其持續時間的長短。

2. 風災：孟加拉灣海域的熱帶氣旋所挾帶的強風、豪雨、大浪，造成孟加拉嚴重的風災、水患。

55. **B**

【解析】 由圖可知甲國製造部門，因生產技術的成熟和產品的標準化，市場價格急遽下降，壓縮了生產的利潤，廠商乃逐漸將製造部門移往廉價勞工眾多的新興工業國（乙、丙國）設廠，但甲國仍保持母國生產的特色，形成「區位擴散」現象。

56. **B**

【解析】 乙為撒赫爾地區，位撒哈拉沙漠和莽原的過渡地帶，自然環境脆弱：北部降水變率較大，以游牧為主。南部降

水較穩定，農牧並行，種植糧食作物。

甲位亞特拉斯山北麓的地中海沿岸→地中海型農業。

丙為剛果盆地→採集、游耕。

丁為南非東南→夏雨型暖溼氣候，商業性農牧業。

57. **A**

【解析】(丁) 屏東墾丁洋蔥栽培面積的變化，無法從臺灣等高線地形圖得知；「圖例」中亦不包括洋蔥。

58-59 為題組

58. **B**

【解析】活動沙丘是因地表植被覆蓋稀，沙源豐富，受風力吹拂而移動的沙丘。

59. **A**

【解析】(B) 乾燥地區沙丘植被稀少，有機質層（O層）不明顯。

(C) 乾燥地區土壤化育成熟度較低，分層較不明顯。

(D) 乾燥地區雨量較少，淋溶作用弱，碳酸鈣等物質聚積，鈣化作用明顯，土壤多為鹼性土。

60-61 為題組

60. **D**

【解析】1. 圖中冬小麥：秋種（3、4、5月），冬季生長（6、7、8、9月），春收（10、11月），可判斷農場位南半球。

2. 兼營小麥和羊毛可知為澳洲東南部的混合農業。

61. D

【解析】 丁：爲玉米帶（混合農業）。

甲：爲放牧帶。

乙：爲棉花帶。

丙：爲酪農帶。

62-63 爲題組

62. C

【解析】 1. 表4中國三大經濟地帶：甲爲西部地帶、乙爲東部沿
海地帶、丙爲中部地帶。

2. 新三大地帶：丁爲中部及近西部區、戊爲遠西部區、
己爲東北及東部區。

※ 本題「三大經濟地帶」之東部沿海地帶及「新三大地帶」
之東北及東部區，分別在「甲、乙、丙」、「丁、戊、
己」中選擇第一級產業比例最低，第三級產業比例最高地
帶即可。

63. D

【解析】 1. 南水北調中線：從長江三峽水庫調水至漢水丹江口水
庫，沿華北平原西緣 輸水至河南、河北、北京、天
津等地。

2. 中線調水路線穿越：中部地帶、東部沿海地帶，和中
部及近西部區、東北及東部區。

64-66 爲題組

64. A

【解析】 牡丹社位於屏東縣境，故搭乘甲路公車。

65. **D 或 C**

　　【解析】　丙（台中－水里）、丁（花蓮火車站－梨山）兩路公車
　　　　　　　皆有行駛台中市境（梨山屬台中市轄區）。

66. **D**

　　【解析】　由雲林出發，順時針方向環島，先後順序路線：丙乙丁甲
　　　　　　　丙：台中－水里（南投）。
　　　　　　　乙：南寮（新竹）－竹科。
　　　　　　　丁：花蓮火車站－梨山（台中）。
　　　　　　　甲：恆春（屏東）－鵬園。

67-69 為題組

67. **A**

　　【解析】　世界觀光旅遊競爭力最強十國中，除新加坡外皆有冰河
　　　　　　　地形。

68. **C**

　　【解析】　(A) 南海：中國、馬來西亞→55.6 + 24.58 = 80.25。
　　　　　　　(B) 北海：英、德→28.13 + 26.88 = 55.01。
　　　　　　　(C) 地中海：法、西、義、土→76.8 + 52.68 + 43.63 + 2
　　　　　　　　　 = 200.11。
　　　　　　　(D) 加勒比海：美、墨→59.75 + 22.4 = 82.15。

69. **A**

　　【解析】　觀光遊憩業的競爭力和到訪人數前十名國家，除中、馬、
　　　　　　　土、墨四國外，均為人類發展程度指標（HDI）較高的
　　　　　　　國家。

70-72 為題組

70. **B**

【解析】 1. 由經緯度（242450.25N，1212312.06E），判斷
位置應在台灣北部。

2. 台省道 7 甲線為中橫支線，沿行蘭陽溪上游，故知蘭
陽溪流域兩側山脈為：中央山脈（西側）和雪山山脈
（東側）。

71. **C**

【解析】 1. 素描者在高處下望，圖中的河流流向表示：圖下方為
上游，上方為下游。

2. 圖上耕地分布在河流左側，應是由丙地向北北東河流
下游望去。

72. **D**

【解析】 中橫支線蘭陽溪流域河階，以高山蔬菜為主。

(A) 咖啡 (B) 菸草 (C) 鳳梨三項作物主要分布於台灣中南
部。

102 年大學入學學科能力測驗試題
自然考科

第壹部分（佔 80 分）

一、單選題（佔 52 分）

說明：第 1 題至第 26 題，每題均計分。每題有 n 個選項，其中只有一個是正確或最適當的選項，請畫記在答案卡之「選擇題答案區」。各題答對者，得 2 分；答錯、未作答或畫記多於一個選項者，該題以零分計算。

1. 花東海岸有一安山岩質角礫岩海蝕洞，離海平面高約 3 公尺。在此海蝕洞接近頂端位置發現帶狀藤壺和其它貝類化石，化石帶寬度約 50 公分。現生藤壺必須在潮間帶附著在岩石上生長，且此地潮差不超過 1 公尺。此帶狀藤壺和其它貝類化石出現在海蝕洞頂端的原因，最可能與下列何種地質作用有關？
   (A) 海嘯　　　　　　(B) 地殼緩慢抬升　　(C) 隕石撞擊
   (D) 大地震　　　　　(E) 山崩

2. 下列是關於星座盤的敘述：
   甲：適用於北緯 25 度的星座盤，也適用於南緯 25 度，只要上下反轉即可。
   乙：同一緯度、不同經度的兩地，可使用同一星座盤。
   丙：臺灣所使用的星座盤正中心，大致是北極星的位置。
   以下選項何者包含所有正確的敘述？
   (A) 甲、乙、丙　　　(B) 甲、丙　　　　　(C) 乙、丙
   (D) 乙　　　　　　　(E) 甲

3. 臺灣平地四季的氣溫一般約在 10～35°C 的範圍，而海洋表面鹽度
受蒸發或降雨作用而增高或降低，近海河口的鹽度則被河水稀釋。
下列何者是臺灣四周海域離岸十公里外海之表層海水可能的溫度
T(°C) 和鹽度 S（單位為 0/00，代表千分比）？

(A) T = 15；S = 7   (B) T = 25；S = 34

(C) T = 30；S = 3.5   (D) T = 35；S = 30

(E) T = 40；S = 10

4. 下列選項圖中箭矢的方向代表海流流向，箭矢的長度代表海流流
速快慢。何者為臺灣四周海域中最可能的海流概況？

(A)   (B)   (C)   (D)

5. 圖 1 為鋒面系統的示意圖，其中左圖為地面天氣圖上常見的冷鋒
與暖鋒；右圖為沿 PQRS 線的垂直剖面圖，其上的曲線與斜線分
別代表冷暖空氣的交界面。有關 Q、R 兩點的鋒面型態與甲、乙、
丙三個區域的地面空氣相對溫度高低，以下選項何者正確？

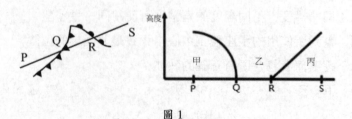

圖 1

選項	Q 點為	R 點為	甲、乙、丙三個區域的地面空氣相對溫度高低
(A)	暖鋒	冷鋒	暖、冷、暖
(B)	暖鋒	冷鋒	冷、暖、暖
(C)	冷鋒	暖鋒	冷、暖、冷
(D)	冷鋒	暖鋒	暖、冷、冷
(E)	冷鋒	暖鋒	暖、暖、冷

6. 下表為甲、乙、丙三種岩石中所含礦物與特徵。此三種岩石是花岡岩、玄武岩與砂岩。已知基性火成岩中不含石英，且火成岩都不具有層理。

岩石	礦物一	礦物二	礦物三	礦物四	礦物五	特徵
甲	石英	正長石	斜長石	白雲母	黑雲母	晶體大而明顯
乙	輝石	斜長石	橄欖石	鈦鐵礦	黃鐵礦	晶體小而不明顯
丙	石英	長石	黏土礦物	方解石	赤鐵礦	有層理

下列有關甲、乙、丙與三種岩石的對應，何者正確？

答案選項	甲	乙	丙
(A)	花岡岩	玄武岩	砂岩
(B)	花岡岩	砂岩	玄武岩
(C)	玄武岩	花岡岩	砂岩
(D)	玄武岩	砂岩	花岡岩
(E)	砂岩	玄武岩	花岡岩

7. 聖嬰現象是一種大氣與海洋的交互作用現象。假設 2022、2024、2026 和 2028 各年的 12 月，赤道東太平洋和赤道西太平洋海平面氣壓異常值（實際氣壓值減三十年長時間氣壓平均值）如表 1：

表 1 12 月海平面氣壓異常值（百帕）

地區	2022 年	2024 年	2026 年	2028 年
赤道東太平洋	+2	-2	+1	-2
赤道西太平洋	+0	-2	-1	+2

哪個選項的 12 月最可能發生聖嬰現象？

(A) 2024　　　　　　(B) 2026　　　　　　(C) 2028

(D) 2022 及 2026　　　(E) 2024 及 2028

8. 太陽表面溫度約為 6000K，氣體大多呈游離狀態。有些微粒可以逃離太陽進入太空，稱為太陽風。下列有關太陽風的描述，何者正確？

(A) 太陽風是現今太陽能的主要來源

(B) 太陽風主要為不帶電的高能粒子

(C) 地球赤道直接面對太陽，受到太陽風的影響最大

(D) 地球南北兩極上空的氣體可受到太陽風撞擊激發，產生極光現象

9. 在生態系物質循環中，下列何種元素不是構成人體內的核酸構造？

(A) 碳　　　(B) 氮　　　(C) 磷　　　(D) 硫　　　(E) 氧

10. 細胞利用呼吸作用以獲得能量，下列有關呼吸作用的敘述，何者正確？

(A) 有氧呼吸的過程中，O_2 會進入粒線體參與作用

(B) 有氧呼吸的過程中，葡萄糖會進入粒線體，然後被分解為丙酮酸

(C) 當細胞內 ADP/ATP 的比值太低時，細胞會加速進行呼吸作用

(D) 當骨骼肌細胞缺氧時，丙酮酸會進入粒線體，然後被分解產

生 ATP

(E) 當酵母菌在缺氧環境下，葡萄糖會進入粒線體，然後被分解產生 ATP

11. 假設某種生物的 DNA 中有五種鹼基，其遺傳密碼子由四個鹼基決定，則該種生物最多能有多少種不同的遺傳密碼子？
　(A) 5^4　　　　　(B) 4^5　　　　　(C) 3^4
　(D) 3^5　　　　　(E) 5^3

12. 基因轉殖是一項重要的生物技術，下列有關基因轉殖技術的敘述，何者正確？
　(A) 目前尚無法成功利用基因轉殖生物做成食品
　(B) 基因轉殖細菌是將重組的 DNA 送入宿主細菌的細胞核
　(C) 目前基因轉殖研究已能成功的將外源基因轉殖入真核細胞中
　(D) 目前已可將胰島素相關外源基因轉殖入糖尿病患者體內，幫助其產生胰島素
　(E) 重組 DNA 技術需先以特定限制酶切開載體 DNA，另以其他種特定限制酶切取欲轉殖的基因，再以 DNA 接合酶（連接酶）重組

13. 科學家挑選與致病病毒具有相同抗原特性的病毒，加以培養，再以高溫或藥劑使其外殼去除活性，經調配後即為「失活病毒疫苗」或稱「致弱病毒疫苗」。僅具有病毒外殼，而不包含遺傳物質的疫苗，稱為「類病毒疫苗」，可大幅降低疫苗注射後的副作用。下列有關病毒與疫苗的敘述，何者錯誤？
　(A) 病毒不具細胞質與胞器
　(B) 病毒由核酸中心與蛋白質外殼組成
　(C) 病毒不具完整的酶素系統，無法獨自製造蛋白質

(D) 「失活病毒疫苗」的蛋白質外殼已變性，但仍然保有抗原的特性

(E) 「類病毒疫苗」僅具病毒外殼，因而不具抗原的特性

14. 探討生物多樣性時，可由遺傳、物種及生態系多樣性等三個層級，加以定性或定量。下列何者為「生態系多樣性」的例子？

(A) 生態池內生產者與各級消費者形成多樣的食物網

(B) 番茄依果實顏色和形狀的差異，可分為 108 個品種（品系）

(C) 樹林內有盤古蟾蜍、澤蛙、面天樹蛙和白頷樹蛙等共 180 隻

(D) 某地區含有草原、灌叢和樹林等各種棲地，其內各具不同物種

(E) 臺灣已發現五種山椒魚、二種蟾蜍、五種小雨蛙、十種樹蛙和十三種赤蛙

15. 下列哪些組的物質，可用來說明倍比定律？

甲：氧與臭氧　　　　　乙：一氧化碳與一氧化氮

丙：水與過氧化氫　　　丁：一氧化氮與二氧化氮

戊：氧化鈣與氫氧化鈣

(A) 甲乙　　(B) 甲丙　　(C) 乙戊　　(D) 丙丁　　(E) 丁戊

16. 下列圖示中，哪些實驗操作正確？

(甲)傾倒液體入量筒　(乙)向試管裡放入粉末　(丙)從瓶裡吸取試劑後　(丁)點燃酒精燈　(戊)收集氫氣

(A) 甲乙　　(B) 甲丙　　(C) 甲戊　　(D) 乙戊　　(E) 丁戊

17. 已知在化學反應 X + 2Y → 3Z + W 中，2 克的 X 能與 4 克的 Y 完全反應，生成 5 克的 Z。若要生成 3 克的W，則需要有多少克的

X 參與反應？

(A) 2　　　　(B) 3　　　　(C) 4　　　　(D) 5　　　　(E) 6

18. 下列有關電子能階的敘述，哪一項錯誤？
    (A) 電子由高能階降至較低能階時，放出的光具有連續頻率
    (B) 氫原子的電子距離原子核愈遠，其能階愈高
    (C) 原子受適當的熱或照光，可使電子躍遷到較高能階
    (D) 霓虹燈的發光係來自原子核外電子的躍遷
    (E) 煙火的焰色來自電子的躍遷

19. 下列哪一種化學反應一定屬於氧化還原反應？
    (A) 結合反應　　　　　　(B) 分解反應
    (C) 酸鹼反應　　　　　　(D) 沉澱反應
    (E) 有元素物質參與的反應

20. 在錐形瓶中的食鹽，緩緩滴入濃 H_2SO_4 溶液，會產生一種氣體。
    下列有關所生成氣體的敘述，何者正確？
    (A) 為淡黃綠色且有刺鼻氣味
    (B) 可用排水集氣法收集
    (C) 此反應為氧化還原反應
    (D) 該氣體的水溶液會侵蝕大理石
    (E) 通入含酚酞的水溶液，則呈現粉紅色

21. 物理學的發展有賴科學家的努力，下列甲至丙所述為物理學發展
    的重要里程碑：
    甲：歸納出行星的運動遵循某些明確的規律
    乙：從電磁場方程式推導出電磁波的速率
    丙：波源與觀察者間的相對速度會影響觀察到波的頻率
    上述發展與各科學家的對應，最恰當的為下列哪一選項？

選項 ＼ 科學家	克卜勒	都卜勒	馬克士威
(A)	甲	乙	丙
(B)	乙	甲	丙
(C)	乙	丙	甲
(D)	丙	甲	乙
(E)	甲	丙	乙

22. 唐朝王維的詩中寫道：「空山不見人，但聞人語響」。在山林中
   看不見人，卻可以聽到樹林間人的對話聲，其原因為下列何者？
   (A) 聲波的速率比光波大，故未見人而先聞聲
   (B) 聲波的能量強度比光波大，故可穿透過樹林傳出
   (C) 聲波的波長與林木間距的尺度較接近，故容易發生繞射而
      傳出
   (D) 聲波的頻率比光波大，故有較大的機率傳到觀察者
   (E) 聲波的波長比光波短，故較容易穿透過樹林傳出

23. 有一固定不動的磁棒及螺線管，磁棒的長軸通過垂直置放之螺線管
   的圓心 P 點，當螺線管
   通以電流時，空間中的
   磁力線分布如圖 2 中的
   虛線。若在圖 2 中 P 點
   右方觀察，則下列關於
   電流與磁場的敘述，何
   者正確？

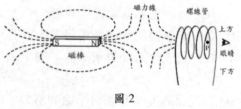

圖 2

   (A) 螺線管上電流為零　　　(B) P 點的磁場方向為向上
   (C) P 點的磁場方向為向下
   (D) 螺線管上電流方向為順時針方向
   (E) 螺線管上電流方向為逆時針方向

24. 下列關於宇宙微波背景輻射的敘述，何者錯誤？
    (A) 它由宇宙中極為稀薄的低溫氣體所發出
    (B) 它現今所對應的溫度比地球南極的年平均溫度還低
    (C) 它現今的強度遠小於家用微波爐烹調食物時內部所產生的微
        波強度
    (D) 它不會對日常生活中的無線電通訊造成明顯的干擾
    (E) 它屬於電磁波

25. 考慮如圖 3 的兩個環形導線，圖中Ⓐ為安培計，若上方導線的電
    流 I_1 隨時間 t 的變化如圖 4 所示：

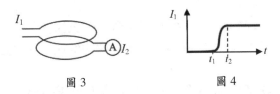

圖 3　　　　　　　　　　圖 4

    試問在下方導線測量到的應電流 I_2 應為下列何者？

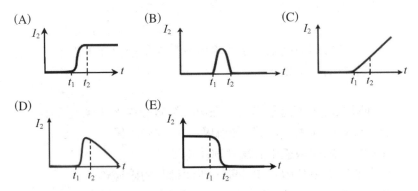

26. 微波爐是利用微波來加熱食物，而微波為波長介於 10^{-4}m 至 0.3m
    間的電磁波。下列何者最適合利用微波爐來加熱？
    (A) 鋁罐裝的運動飲料
    (B) 紙盒內的乾燥香菇

(C) 不銹鋼杯內的茶水

(D) 紙杯內的咖啡飲料

(E) 塑膠盒內的乾燥麵粉

二、多選題（佔 30 分）

說明：第 27 題至第 35 題，每題均計分。每題有 n 個選項，其中至少
有一個是正確的選項，請將正確選項畫記在答案卡之「選擇題
答案區」。各題之選項獨立判定，所有選項均答對者，得 2 分；
答錯 k 個選項者，得該題 n-2k/n 的分數；但得分低於零分或所
有選項均未作答者，該題以零分計算。

27. 臺灣位處歐亞大陸與太平洋的交界地帶，天氣深受季風、梅雨與
颱風的影響。以下關於臺灣常見天氣型態的敘述，哪些正確？
（應選 2 項）

(A) 梅雨是因為暖鋒通過造成的，因此非常潮濕悶熱

(B) 秋天的颱風常引進西南氣流，為東北部山區帶來大量降水

(C) 梅雨和颱風是臺灣南部地區主要的降水來源

(D) 東北季風主要發生在冬季，下雨時常伴隨閃電雷聲

(E) 除了梅雨與颱風，東北季風與夏季午後雷陣雨也是臺灣北部
重要的降水來源

28. 下列哪些現象或過程僅發生在第一減數分裂？（應選 2 項）

(A) 成對的同源染色體互相配對，形成四分體

(B) 紡錘絲由兩組中心體共同產生

(C) 姊妹染色分體互相分離，並向細胞的兩極移動

(D) 細胞核膜、核仁消失

(E) 非同源染色體自由組合

29. 圖 5 為某一家族的紅綠色盲遺傳譜系圖。下列關於此家庭之成員
的視覺以及是否攜帶色盲基因的推論，哪些正確？（應選3項）

(A) 僅有男性成員攜帶色盲基因

(B) 視覺正常但一定攜帶色盲基因的
　　男性成員有三位

(C) 視覺正常但一定攜帶色盲基因的
　　女性成員有三位

(D) 視覺正常但一定<u>不攜帶</u>色盲基因
　　的家族成員有五位

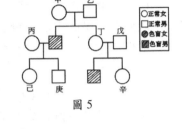

圖 5

(E) 視覺正常但一定攜帶色盲基因的家族成員為甲、丁、己

(F) 視覺正常但一定<u>不攜帶</u>色盲基因的家族成員為乙、戊、庚

30. 用試管取 0.1M 碘化鉀溶液 3mL 後，滴入 0.1M 硝酸鉛溶液 2mL，
　　立即產生沉澱。下列有關該實驗的敘述，哪些正確？（應選 3 項）

(A) 產生的沉澱是白色

(B) 硝酸鉛是限量試劑

(C) 加完 2mL 的硝酸鉛溶液後，再加入碘化鉀溶液，沉澱的量會
　　隨之增加

(D) 實驗完畢，含鉛離子的廢液要歸類為重金屬的廢液回收

(E) 清洗裝過碘化鉀容器的廢液，可以用一般廢液的方式處理

31. 甲為 0.01 M 鹽酸水溶液，將其以純水稀釋一千倍後得水溶液乙，
　　再將乙以純水稀釋一千倍後得水溶液丙，再將丙以純水稀釋一千
　　倍後得水溶液丁。廣用試紙之顏色如表列：

pH	2	3	4	5	6	7	8	9	10	11
顏色	紅	橙紅	橙黃	黃	黃綠	綠	淺藍	深藍	靛	紫

下列有關試紙呈色的敘述，哪些正確？（應選 3 項）

(A) 甲溶液使廣用試紙呈紅色　　(B) 乙溶液使廣用試紙呈黃色

(C) 丙溶液使廣用試紙呈淺藍色　(D) 丁溶液使廣用試紙呈紫色

(E) 甲溶液使藍色石蕊試紙呈紅色

32. 光電效應是光具有粒子性的實驗證據，今以單色光照射金屬表面後，金屬表面的電子吸收入射光的能量，部分能量用於克服金屬表面對電子的束縛，剩餘能量則轉為電子動能，自金屬表面逸出，成為光電子。下列有關此光電效應實驗的敘述，哪些正確？（應選 2 項）

    (A) 入射光子的能量由頻率決定，頻率越高，能量越大
    (B) 入射光子的能量由光強度決定，強度越大，頻率越高
    (C) 入射光子的頻率越高，光電子的動能會隨之增加
    (D) 入射光的強度越大，光電子的動能會隨之增加
    (E) 以同一單色光照射時，光電子的動能與被照金屬材料的種類無關

33. 質子和中子能組成穩定的原子核結構，下列哪些選項是其主要原因？（應選 3 項）

    (A) 質子和質子間的電磁力　　　(B) 質子和中子間的電磁力
    (C) 質子和質子間的強作用力　　(D) 質子和中子間的強作用力
    (E) 中子和中子間的強作用力　　(F) 中子和中子間的弱作用力

34. 歐洲核子研究組織於 2012 年 7 月宣布探測到極可能是希格斯玻色子的新粒子，但有待確認。希格斯玻色子是「標準模型」可預測出的一種基本粒子，是一種不帶電荷且不穩定的粒子。根據希格斯假說，希格斯場遍佈於宇宙，有些基本粒子因為與希格斯場交互作用而獲得質量，希格斯場就像是一池膠水，會黏著於某些基本粒子，使粒子具有質量。假若進一步的實驗確認了希格斯玻色子的存在，則可以支持「標準模型」的理論，也可給予希格斯假說極大的肯定，特別是對於解釋為什麼有些基本粒子具有質量。根據上文，下列敘述哪些正確？（應選 2 項）

    (A) 希格斯玻色子是已被確認的最新一種基本粒子
    (B) 希格斯玻色子是相對論中預測必然存在的一種基本粒子

(C) 若希格斯玻色子存在，則可用來解釋有些基本粒子何以具有質量

(D) 若希格斯玻色子經實驗證實存在，則可支持「標準模型」的理論

(E) 標準模型所預測的希格斯玻色子具有質量，帶有電量

35. 臺灣全島地形複雜，雖然雨量豐沛但是分布相當不均勻。颱風帶來的降雨是臺灣重要的水資源，但是颱風也常帶來洪水災害。2010 年 10 月 21 日梅姬颱風侵台之際，正值東北季風盛行，當天宜蘭各地出現強降雨現象，部分地區更因地勢低窪，且 24 小時內累積雨量達 432 毫米，已達超大豪雨標準，致使水淹路面，人車受阻。試參考梅姬颱風路徑（圖 6），選出正確敘述。（應選 2 項）

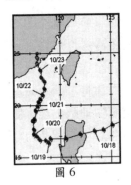

圖 6

(A) 因為颱風環流與東北季風共伴效應，致使宜蘭地區降下超大豪雨

(B) 因為颱風引發強烈西南氣流，致使宜蘭地區降下超大豪雨

(C) 因為宜蘭地區位於迎風面，降雨量大

(D) 因為宜蘭位於颱風外圍環流下降處，降雨量暴增

(E) 此報導有誤，宜蘭一天的累積雨量不可能超過 400 毫米

三、綜合題（佔 10 分）

說明：第 36 題至第 40 題，每題 2 分，每題均計分，請將正確選項畫記在答案卡之「選擇題答案區」。單選題答錯、未作答或畫記多於一個選項者，該題以零分計算：多選題每題有 n 個選項，答錯 k 個選項者，得該題 $\frac{n-2k}{n}$ 的分數；但得分低於零分或所有選項均未作答者，該題以零分計算。

<u>36~40 爲題組</u>

地球表面有 70% 以上的面積被水覆蓋著，天然水中除雨水比較純淨外，其他的天然水均溶有鹽類或其他雜質。水的淨化以及水污染的防治爲目前開發水資源的重要課題。

水對核能發電很重要，可以吸收核分裂時所釋放出的能量，生成高溫的水蒸氣以推動發電機。核反應機組也需要使用大量的冷卻水將餘熱帶走，才不會讓核心溫度持續升高，釀成災變，這也是核能發電廠大多建在海邊的緣故。

生命也離不開水，在動植物組織中，水是最豐富的物質。細胞可藉由滲透作用得到或喪失水分，例如植物細胞中，由於細胞壁和細胞質間滲透性的差異，所以當細胞外濃度高於內部時，因水分從液胞（泡）中流失，使植物細胞出現細胞壁與細胞膜互相剝離的情形（如圖 7），稱爲「質離現象」。

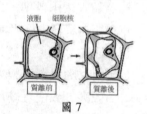
圖 7

36. 下列關於滲透的敘述，哪些正確？（應選 2 項）
　(A) 滲透是活細胞才會有的現象
　(B) 低濃度溶液的水，因滲透到高濃度溶液中，以致體積減少
　(C) 溶液中，水與溶質通過半透膜的移動稱爲滲透
　(D) 通過細胞膜的滲透作用，有時可藉由運輸蛋白提高效率
　(E) 滲透作用均需要消耗能量

37. 將植物細胞持續浸泡在蔗糖溶液中，使其出現「質離現象」，約在 10 分鐘後達到平衡狀態，即植物細胞的細胞質體積已不再變化。下列相關敘述，哪些正確？（應選 3 項）
　(A) 蔗糖溶液對該植物細胞而言爲高張溶液

(B) 浸泡之初，水分子的淨移動方向爲由細胞外向細胞內

(C) 浸泡之初至細胞出現質離現象的過程中，細胞內滲透壓持續變大

(D) 細胞內外的滲透壓達到平衡時，水分子仍然經細胞膜進行移動

(E) 細胞內外的滲透壓達到平衡時，液胞內充滿了蔗糖溶液

38. 下列有關自來水的敘述，哪些正確？（應選 3 項）

(A) 自來水加氯消毒是利用氯氣的還原反應能力

(B) 臭氧可用於自來水消毒，是利用其具有強氧化力的特性

(C) 要去除湖水、雨水等水中的雜質，是靠離心力

(D) 在混濁的水中加入明礬使水澄清，是一種沉澱反應

(E) 自來水加氯消毒後仍保持些許餘氯，可利用煮沸的方式去除大部分餘氯

39. 下列有關工業廢水處理過程的敘述，哪些正確？（應選 3 項）

(A) 在處理工業廢水的第一步，常加入碳酸鈉使廢水的 pH 值小於 7

(B) 工業廢水常含重金屬離子，在強鹼的條件下會產生沉澱，可用過濾法分離

(C) 工業廢水用鹼處理後的鹼性溶液，必須要用醋酸將其調成中性後，始可放流

(D) 去除重金屬離子後的中性廢水，可灑成水幕來曝氣，以增加水中的溶氧

(E) 可利用有細菌的活性污泥，讓細菌來消化有機物，以達淨水目的

40. 核能發電反應機組停機後,核分裂連鎖反應會停止,但是反應後的產物仍具有放射性,也會持續產生餘熱而造成高溫。若停機後的餘熱發電功率為 P_r,核能機組正常發電功率為 P,以 P_r/P $= W$ 為縱軸,則其隨時間改變的曲線如圖 8 所示。假設核電廠某一機組正常發電功率為每小時 64 萬度,而某用戶每個月用電度數為 320 度,則停機經過一天後,該時的餘熱用來發電一小時的電能,與該用戶用電約多久時間的電能相等?

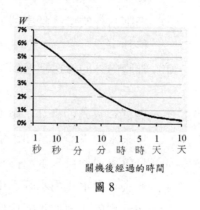

圖 8

(A) 3小時   (B) 3天   (C) 30天

(D) 300天   (E) 3000天

第貳部分 (佔 48 分)

說明: 第 41 題至第 68 題,每題 2 分。單選題答錯、未作答或畫記多於一個選項者,該題以零分計算;多選題每題有 n 個選項,答錯 k 個選項者,得該題 n-2k/n 的分數;但得分低於零分或所有選項均未作答者,該題以零分計算。此部分得分超過 48 分以上,以滿分 48 分計。

41. 衛星雲圖是氣象觀測重要工具之一,常見的有可見光雲圖和紅外線雲圖,分別可知雲層的厚薄和高低。圖 9 為某年 11 月初的衛星影像,在黃海附近有寒潮爆發所形成條狀排列的雲(圖中丙處),同時南方有兩個明顯的熱帶低壓(圖中甲、乙兩處)。利用此二幅衛星影像判斷,以下的敘述何者正確?

圖 9

(A) 甲處的雲，為兩熱帶低壓的外圍環流合併所致，發展得又高又濃密

(B) 乙處的雲，在可見光或者紅外線都很明顯，顯示它是又厚又高的雲

(C) 丙處的雲為對流發展旺盛的積雨雲，所以在可見光雲圖較明顯，而紅外線雲圖較暗淡

(D) 甲處的雲主要是低層雲，所以在可見光雲圖較黯淡，而紅外線雲圖較明顯

(E) 乙處的雲主要是高層雲，所以在可見光雲圖較明顯，而紅外線雲圖較暗淡

42. 現代海洋研究船在現場測量海水鹽度時，是使用溫鹽深儀（CTD）。此儀器是測量海水的哪一項數值，而後再換算為海水鹽度？

(A) 導電度　　　　(B) 穩定度　　　　(C) 濁度
(D) 氯度　　　　　(E) 密度

43. 植物運動的機制，可能是因器官內的細胞有不同生長速率，或者有不同的膨壓變化所造成。下列哪一項運動的機制與其他四項的機制不同？

(A) 胡瓜的卷鬚會纏繞棚架

(B) 玉米橫放的根會向地心方向延伸

(C) 大豆的葉片在夜間會閉合起來

(D) 綠豆的莖頂會朝橫向光源方向生長

(E) 禾草的芽鞘由基部向上生長

44. 圖 10 橫軸中的甲~戊為某陸域生態系中的五種生物，構成包含生產者及各級消費者的一條完整食物鏈；縱軸為各生物族群所含的總能量。下列相關敘述何者正確？

(A) 甲為第二營養階層

(B) 乙的個體數一定最多

(C) 丙為第四級消費者

(D) 丁一定為肉食性動物

(E) 戊為生產者

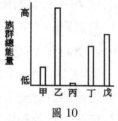

圖 10

45. 生存在某地區的物種，在消長過程中，原有群集內的優勢物種，其地位可能會被其他物種所取代。在某群集經歷森林大火後的消長過程中，甲、乙和丙為三種植物，其優勢物種改變順序為甲→乙→丙，若選項中各圖的縱軸為物種個體數，橫軸為時間，則群集中生物組成的改變情形，下列何者最為可能？

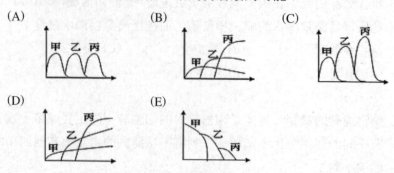

(A)　　　　　　　(B)　　　　　　　(C)

(D)　　　　　　　(E)

46～47 為題組

　　傍晚天色剛暗時，往西方低空偶見金星與木星雙星拱月的天象，形成微笑的模樣（如圖 11，圖片拍攝於臺北）。

46. 下列相關敘述哪些正確？（應選 3 項）

圖 11

(A) 該圖的拍攝日期可能為農曆初四

(B) 該圖的拍攝日期可能為農曆二十六日

(C) 此時三者到地球距離的比較為：
金星＞木星＞月亮

(D) 此時三者到地球距離的比較為：
木星＞金星＞月亮

(E) 月亮在圖中的移動方向可能是朝右下方

(F) 月亮在圖中的移動方向可能是朝左下方

47. 當時月亮仰角約 17 度，金星仰角約 19 度，木星仰角約 20 度。一天後的同一時間在同一地點進行觀察，則下列何者為可能發生的現象？

(A) 月亮與金星、木星間的夾角變大，且之後月亮落於地平面下的時間比前一天早

(B) 三者間的相對位置不變，但是之後月亮落於地平面下的時間比前一天早

(C) 三者間的相對位置不同，但是之後月亮落於地平面下的時間與前一天相同

(D) 三者間的相對位置及之後月亮落於地平面下的時間皆不會改變

(E) 月亮的仰角大於金星和木星的仰角

48. 下列有關 H_2O、CO_2、SiO_2、MgO、Ca、Si、Br_2 等 7 種物質，其在常溫常壓下的性質與構造的敘述，何者正確？
    (A) 有 1 個物質為液體
    (B) 有 2 個物質為氣體
    (C) 有 3 個物質為固體
    (D) 有 2 個物質為網狀固體

49. 在選項所列有機物中，哪兩種符合下列條件？（應選 2 項）
    甲：生活中較常見的有機物
    乙：屬於烷烴的衍生物
    丙：分子只由碳、氫、氧三種元素構成
    (A) 乙醇　　　　　　　(B) 乙胺　　　　　　　(C) 乙酸
    (D) 核酸　　　　　　　(E) 胺基酸

50. 在硝酸銀和硝酸銅的混合溶液中，加入少量的鐵粉並充分反應後，有少量的金屬析出，過濾後得金屬 M 與濾液 L。取少量 L，滴入食鹽水後得白色沉澱。試由此推測所析出的 M 是什麼金屬，以及濾液 L 中含有什麼金屬離子？

選項	(A)	(B)	(C)	(D)	(E)
M	Cu	Cu	Cu、Ag	Ag	Ag
L	Ag^+	Ag^+、Cu^{2+}、Fe^{2+}	Ag^+、Fe^{2+}	Cu^{2+}	Ag^+、Cu^{2+}、Fe^{2+}

51. 在光滑水平面上一質量 M 的質點以 2.0m/s 的速率向右運動，與靜止的另一質量 $4M$ 的質點發生一維非彈性碰撞。碰撞後質量 M 的質點反彈，以速率 0.50m/s 向左運動，則質量 $4M$ 質點碰撞後向右的速率約為多少？
    (A) 0　　　　　　　　　(B) 0.38m/s　　　　　　(C) 0.63m/s
    (D) 0.94m/s　　　　　　(E) 2.5m/s

52～53 為題組

　　美國國家航空暨太空總署發射的「好奇號」火星探測車，於 2012 年 8 月成功降落在火星的隕石坑。火星一直是人類太空探測的重點目標，期望「好奇號」的火星之旅能憑藉先進科學儀器的探索，獲得解答生命疑問的線索。

52. 下列關於探測火星的敘述，何者正確？
    (A) 火星與月球一樣是地球的衛星，是目前看來最適合人類移居的星體
    (B) 火星是太陽系中最鄰近地球且較地球靠近太陽的行星，因此較可能存在生命
    (C) 火星與地球一樣具有相同的繞日週期，因此有相似的季節變化
    (D) 火星與地球一樣具有衛星，因此有相似的晝夜變化
    (E) 火星繞日軌跡為橢圓，公轉一圈的時間大於地球上的一年

53. 已知地球的平均半徑約為火星的 1.9 倍，地球的質量約為火星的 9.3 倍。若忽略空氣阻力，而將同一小球以相同的初速度分別於火星表面與地球表面鉛直上拋，則小球在空中運動的時間，在火星上約為地球上的多少倍？
    (A) 0.20　　(B) 0.38　　(C) 1.0　　(D) 2.6　　(E) 4.9

54～55 為題組

　　物體自高處落下時，除了受到重力之外，還有空氣阻力。某同學觀測一小物體自高處落下，其速度 v 與時間 t 的關係如圖 12。

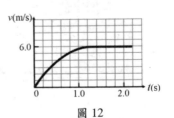

圖 12

54. 圖 12 的數據中，小物體從 $t = 0$s 至 $t = 2.0$s 的位移與下列何值
（單位為 m）最為接近？

(A) 4　　　　(B) 6　　　　(C) 9　　　　(D) 12　　　　(E) 14

55. 下列有關小物體運動的敘述，何者正確？

(A) 小物體的加速度量值越來越大

(B) 在 $t = 1.4$s 時，小物體所受空氣阻力的量值為零

(C) 在落下的全程中，小物體所受空氣阻力的量值為一定值

(D) 小物體所受空氣阻力的量值隨速率增快而變大

(E) 在 $t = 2.0$s時，小物體所受重力量值為零

56. 日本本島位於北美洲板塊，2011 年 3 月 11 日在日本東北近海發
生規模 9.0 的地震，此地震發生在日本海溝的隱沒板塊上，星號
代表震央位置。由設在日本本州島上的全球衛星定位系統（GPS）
地面觀測站可以測得伴隨地震發生後的地殼變形，稱為同震變形。
圖 13 為水平同震變形（左圖）和垂直同震變形（右圖），右圖中
箭頭向上表示抬升，箭頭向下表示沉降，圖上灰色部分表示陸地，
白色部分表示海洋。下列有關日本近海地震的敘述，哪些正確？
（應選 2 項）

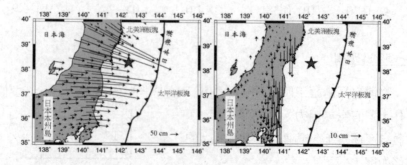

圖 13

(A) 此地震是由逆斷層活動所造成

(B) 島上東側大都顯示同震沉降，所以此地震是由正斷層活動所造成

(C) 島上水平同震位移大多往東移動，所以北美洲板塊向東隱沒在太平洋板塊之下

(D) 島上水平同震位移大多往東移動，所以太平洋板塊向西隱沒在北美洲板塊之下

(E) 島上最大水平同震位移量可達 15m

57. 圖 14 為某小島的簡易地形圖，等高線上的數字表示海拔高度，單位為公尺，已知全島由沉積岩層所組成，山頂上的長線表示岩層走向，短線表示岩層傾斜的方向，旁邊的數字表示岩層的傾斜角度，圖中哪一選項的區域為順向坡？

(A) 甲區

(B) 乙區

(C) 丙區

(D) 丙區及丁區

(E) 乙區及丙區

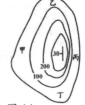

圖 14

58. 下列哪些屬於人體的「專一性防禦」？（應選 2 項）

(A) 胃黏膜的防衛作用　　(B) 皮膚的阻隔作用

(C) 發炎反應　　(D) 器官移植的排斥

(E) 抗流感病毒的抗體作用

59. 下列人體的器官或構造，哪些不是藉由具有較大的表面積來加速物質的吸收或交換？（應選 2 項）

(A) 微血管　　(B) 大腸　　(C) 皮膚

(D) 肺泡　　(E) 小腸絨毛

60. 下表選項中有關人體動脈、靜脈及微血管的構造及心週期之壓力變化的比較，哪些正確？（應選 2 項）

選項	比較內容	動脈	靜脈	微血管
(A)	內皮細胞	有	有	無
(B)	平滑肌	有	無	有
(C)	瓣膜	無	有	無
(D)	管壁含有結締組織	有	無	無
(E)	心週期中的壓力變化	最大	最小	中間

61. 科學家在 1996～2001 年間，調查惠蓀林場中「斯文豪氏赤蛙」的族群數量變化，調查期間歷經集集大地震。這些科學家先在隨機捕獲的赤蛙身上植入晶片做標記後將之野放，再於每月首日重新捕捉，以估算其族群數量，記錄結果如圖 15。記錄分為 3 類，分別為「再捕捉」：先前曾被捕捉過的個體，身上已植有晶片；「新捕捉」：新捕捉到的個體，其身上沒有晶片；「逃跑」：只聽到聲音或看到但無法捉到之個體，無法判斷是否植有晶片。地震前後斯文豪氏赤蛙族群動態的描述，哪些正確？（應選 3 項）

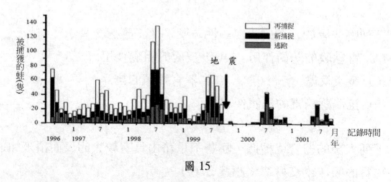

圖 15

(A) 地震後青蛙數量明顯下降

(B) 地震後「再捕捉」個體的比例顯著降低甚至消失

(C) 地震後的族群，多為地震前存活下來的個體所組成

(D) 地震後的族群，多由新個體所組成，地震前的個體多已消失

(E) 地震後青蛙的數量，主要集中出現在春夏兩季，秋冬時甚至可能完全消失

62～63 為題組

　　共價化合物通常是由幾種非金屬元素結合而成；離子化合物通常是由金屬元素和非金屬元素結合而成。

62. X、Y 是位於相差一個週期的兩個元素，且原子序均小於 20，其離子的價電子層相差兩層。已知 Y 的原子序大於 X 的原子序，且 Y 是由共價鍵結合成的元素。試由此推測下列敘述，哪些正確？（應選 2 項）

(A) Y 是非金屬元素

(B) X 容易成為陰離子

(C) X 離子由內層到外層的電子數為 2、8、8

(D) Y 離子的電子數可為 2

(E) Y 可以屬於第 3 週期

63. 今有價電子數為 1 的原子 Q 與價電子數為 6 的原子 R，且 Q 與 R 的原子序均小於 20，則由其結合而成的化合物型態，有哪些可能？（應選 2 項）

(A) Q_2R 型共價化合物　　(B) QR_2 型離子化合物

(C) QR_6 型共價化合物　　(D) QR_2 型共價化合物

(E) Q_2R 型離子化合物　　(F) QR_6 型離子化合物

64~65 為題組

64. 將等重量的 NaNO$_3$ 與 KNO$_3$
充分均勻混合後，另取一個
醇類化合物為溶劑，進行混
合物的溶解度量測實驗，量
測結果如圖 16 所示，其縱軸
為 100 克溶劑中溶質的克數。
下列敘述，哪些正確？
（應選 2 項）

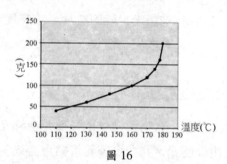

圖 16

(A) 在 160°C 時，100 克的溶液溶有 50 克的溶質

(B) 在 160°C 時，100 克的溶液溶有 100 克的溶質

(C) 在 160°C 時，100 克的溶劑溶有 100 克的溶質

(D) 在 120°C 時，KNO$_3$ 的重量百分濃度約為 50%

(E) 充分均勻混合後的溶質為等莫耳數的 NaNO$_3$ 與 KNO$_3$

65. 溶解度與溶質—溶質、溶質—溶劑、溶劑—溶劑間的作用力有關。
下列敘述，哪些正確？（應選 2 項）

(A) KNO$_3$ 晶體中的結合力為靜電作用力

(B) 此溶劑分子之間具有共價鍵

(C) 若將 KNO$_3$ 及 NaNO$_3$ 溶於水後，大部分以 KNO$_3$ 及 NaNO$_3$
的形式存在

(D) 在 110~160°C 範圍內，溶質—溶劑間作用力的屬性改變了

(E) 造成在 170°C 以後的現象，其可能原因為溶質—溶劑間的作
用力屬性劇烈改變

66～67 為題組

16 世紀伽利略設計了一個
光滑沒有阻力的斜坡道實
驗，如圖 17 所示。左邊的
坡道斜度是固定的，但是
右邊坡道的斜度與長度不
同，甲為最陡坡道，丁為
一假想情境，沒有任何坡
度且可水平的展延到無窮
遠處。將一小球分別在
甲、乙、丙、丁四個坡道

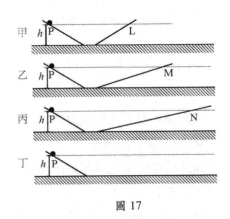

圖 17

由高度為 h 的 P 點靜止放下，實驗發現，在甲、乙、丙三個坡
道，球最後都可以到達高度相同的 L、M、N 三個點，且與球
的質量無關。

66. 根據上文，下列敘述哪些正確？（應選 2 項）

(A) 在坡道底部，較重的球比較輕的球滑動速度較快

(B) 在坡道底部，較輕的球比較重的球滑動速度較快

(C) 不同質量的球所受的重力都相同

(D) 球經由丁坡道滑下後會維持等速度前進，不會停下來

(E) 利用丁坡道的想像實驗可推論出動者恆動的說法

67. 上文所描述的運動過程中，下列哪些物理量不會隨時間發生改
變？（應選 2 項）

(A) 甲坡道上球的重力位能

(B) 乙坡道上球的動能

(C) 丙坡道上球的力學能

(D) 丁坡道上球的重力位能

(E) 丁坡道上球的力學能

68. 王同學到臺東太麻里野外調查，觀察南北向剖面上的褶皺構造如圖18，經詳細調查後，地層層序由1到5愈來愈年輕，判斷褶皺構造時需考量地層年代的排列。對於這個褶皺構造的敘述，下列何者正確？

(A) 地層沒倒轉，褶皺構造是背斜

(D) 地層已倒轉，褶皺構造是背斜

(C) 地層沒倒轉，褶皺構造是向斜

(D) 地層已倒轉，褶皺構造是向斜

(E) 褶皺兩翼岩層的傾向為同一方向

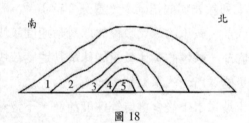

圖 18

102年度學科能力測驗自然科試題詳解

第壹部分

一、單選題

1. **B 或 D**

   【解析】 海洋生物化石出現於陸地上，表發生的原因爲陸地上
   升或海平面下降；故應選 (B) 選項；但由於地殼在變
   動的過程中會產生地震，故 (D) 選項有爭議；因此本
   題 (B)(D) 均給分。

2. **C**

   【解析】 星座盤的中心乃是地球的自轉軸，因此中心的位置應
   爲各地的自轉軸方向。因爲台灣位於北半球，故中心
   位置爲天北極，接近目前北極星位置。此外，星座盤
   乃是在各地不同緯度所觀測的天球範圍，因此只要緯
   度相同均適用同一星座盤。

3. **B**

   【解析】 台灣位副熱帶氣候類型，氣溫可達 35℃，但由於水的
   比熱較大，因此水溫較氣溫低；所以 (D)(E) 兩選項必
   定錯誤。此外，海水的平均鹽度約爲 35 $^0/_{00}$；所以
   (A)(C) 兩選項必爲錯誤，答案故選 (B)。

4. **B**

   【解析】 台灣洋流系統主要受季風與行星風系影響；故在冬夏
   兩季的洋流系統有所差異。其中夏季在台灣的東部外
   海主要有黑潮的主流流經，而黑潮在流經恆春半島時，

部分海水受地形影響形成黑潮支流進入台灣海峽；但
由於是支流，故水流量與流速均較主流慢，因此答案
選 (B)。

5. **C**

【解析】 冷鋒的標誌與暖鋒的標誌分別為三角形與半圓形；其
中三角形與半圓形分別意指冷空氣與暖空氣前進的方
向。因此冷鋒表甲為冷空氣下沉至暖空氣下方 (乙)；
而暖鋒表暖空氣 (乙) 上升至冷空氣 (丙) 上方，故丙為
冷空氣。

6. **A**

【解析】 花崗岩為酸性岩漿表 SiO2 含量大，故其主要組成礦物
以長石、石英為主；再加上為深成岩表冷卻速度慢，
礦物結晶顆粒大，故為甲。玄武岩為基性岩漿表 SiO2
含量少；礦物大多為輝石、角閃石、橄欖石為主；再
加上為火山岩表冷卻速度快結晶顆粒小，故為乙。
砂岩為經過外營力長久搬運後堆積的岩石，故礦物
組成大多為硬度較高的礦物如石英；再加上為沉積
岩具備層理；故為丙。

7. **C**

【解析】 聖嬰現象是一種氣候異常的現象，常發生於聖誕節前
後；主要的原因是太平洋東西兩側的氣壓值變化，造
成赤道東風減弱，進而影響洋流與氣候。聖嬰年發
生時東太平洋氣壓減弱；西岸增強，故選 (C)。

8. **D**

【解析】 (A) 太陽能來自光能，非太陽風之帶電粒子。

(B) 主要為帶電粒子。

(C) 帶電粒子會受地磁影響，因此太陽風對赤道影響非常大。

9. **D**

【解析】 核酸構成的元素有碳、氫、氧、氮、磷不含硫；硫是蛋白質組成元素，不是核酸。

10. **A**

【解析】 有氧呼吸分為三大步驟：糖解作用、克氏循環、電子傳遞鏈。其中只有在粒線體進行的電子傳遞鏈需要氧氣參與，故選 (A)。

(B) 葡萄糖需先分解為丙酮酸後，才能進入粒線體繼續進行分解作用。

(C) ADP/ATP 比值小，表示細胞的 ATP 多，所以會促進細胞進行耗能的合成作用。

(D) 骨骼肌缺氧時，會將丙酮酸硫在細胞質進行還原作用，轉為乳酸。

(E) 酵母菌缺氧時會將丙酮酸硫在細胞質轉變為酒精和二氧化碳。

11. **A**

【解析】 四個含氮鹽基組成遺傳密碼，表示有四個含氮鹽基的填入位，當五種含氮鹽基時，則每一個位置都有 5 種可能選擇，因此總共會有 5 的四次方種可能組合 ($5 \times 5 \times 5 \times 5 = 5^4$)，故應選 (A)。

12. **C**

【解析】 (A) 已有基改大豆、玉米上市。

   (B) 細菌沒有細胞核，是將基因轉殖到細菌的質體
     DNA 上。

   (C) 現在已經有可以製造人類凝血因子的基因轉殖羊。

   (D) 目前尚無法將胰島素基因轉殖到人體，只有基因
     轉殖細菌。

   (E) 必須利用相同的限制酵素來切開質體與欲轉殖基
     因，這樣才能產生相同的單股末端，來進行 DNA
     的接合與重組。

13. **E**

 【解析】(E) 病毒的蛋白質外殼上必須具有病毒的抗原分子，
     也必須具有抗原性，否則不能用來活化淋巴球，
     誘導抗體形成。

   【病毒特性】不具有細胞結構，沒有酵素系統，不能
  獨立進行代謝作用，無法獨立製造蛋白質，為絕對寄
  生的病原體，只有在寄主細胞內才能進行唯一的生命
  現象——繁殖。

14. **D**

 【解析】生物多樣性分為三個層級：

   1. 遺傳多樣性強調同一物種個體內的遺傳變異。

   2. 物種多樣性強調物種的豐富度和均勻度。

   3. 生態系多樣性強調棲地提供給生物生存資源的能力。

   (A) 敘述的是食物鏈、食物網的形成。

   (B) 強調遺傳多樣性。

   (C) (E) 強調物種多樣性。

15. **D**

 【解析】倍比定律：若兩元素可以生成兩種或兩種以上的化合

物時，一元素質量固定，則另一元素的質量成簡單整
數比⇒找有兩種元素的化合物∴丙、丁。

16. **A**
　【解析】(丙) 滴管不可倒置
　　　　　(丁) 酒精燈不可以用來點燃另一個酒精燈
　　　　　(戊) 排水集氣。

17. **E**
　【解析】根據質量守恆定律 ⇒2+4=5+W⇒W=1　2:1=X:3⇒X=6

18. **A**
　【解析】不連續光譜⇒不連續頻率

19. **E**
　【解析】(E) 一定有氧化數改變

20. **D**
　【解析】$2NaCl+H_2SO_4 \to 2HCl+Na_2SO_4$ 產生的氣體 HCl
　　　　　(A) 描述的是 Cl_2
　　　　　(B) HCl 易溶於水，不能用排水集氣法收集
　　　　　(C) 複分解反應
　　　　　(D) 大理石含 $CaCO_3$，遇酸產生 CO_2
　　　　　(E) 無色

21. **E**
　【解析】甲→克卜勒三大行星運動定律
　　　　　乙→馬克士威電磁方程
　　　　　丙→都卜勒效應

22. **C**

【解析】 (A) 光波波速>聲波波速

(B) 無關

(D) (E) 因爲繞射

23. **D**

【解析】 (A) 不爲零

(B) (C) 方向向左

(D) (E) 順時針

24. **A**

【解析】 宇宙早期的熱輻射隨宇宙膨脹溫度不斷降低

25. **B**

【解析】 感應電流來自磁場變化，電流變化會產生磁場變化

26. **D**

【解析】 不能有金屬，且要含水

二、多選題

27. **CE**

【解析】 (A) 梅雨是滯留鋒面；

(B) 秋颱造成共伴效應，使得東北部降豪大雨；

(D) 冬季的東北季風降雨主要以地形雨爲主，雨勢較小，並不會伴隨閃電。

28. **AE**

【解析】 (A) 成對的同源染色體互相配對發生第一次減數分裂的前期，即聯會。

(B)(D) 有絲分裂與減數分裂都會產生。

(C) 有絲分裂與第二次減數分裂都會產生。

(E) 非同源染色體自由組合，即為孟德爾第二定律的自由配合律。

29. **CEF**

【解析】 圖中每個人的基因型如下圖所示：

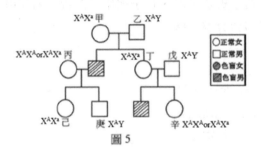

圖5

(A) 女性亦可攜帶色盲基因；

(B) 男性若有色盲基因則必為色盲。

(D) 視覺正常但一定不帶有色盲基因者有乙、戊、庚三位。

30. **CDE**

【解析】 (A) 產生沉澱 PbI_2 是黃色的

(B) $\dfrac{0.1 \times 3}{2} < 0.2$，限量試劑是 $KI_{(aq)}$

31. **ABE**

【解析】 甲：0.01M，乙：$0.01M \times 10^{-3} = 10^{-5}$，

丙：$10^{-5} \times 10^{-3} = 10^{-8}$，丁：$10^{-8} \times 10^{-3} = 10^{-11}$

(A) pH = 2　　　　　(B) pH = 5

(C)(D) pH 接近 7　　　(E) 仍為酸性→紅色

32. **AC**

【解析】(B) 請看 (A)，$E = hf$，f 為光的頻率

(C) 光電方程：$E_{光子} = 動函數 + E_{光電子}$

(D) 入射光的頻率愈高，光電子的動能隨之增加

(E) 各金屬功函數不同

33. **CDE**

【解析】質子與質子間、質子與中子間皆為強作用力，弱作用力與衰變有關

34. **CD**

【解析】(A) 非已確認

(B) 非相對論

(E) 不帶電

35. **AC**

【解析】(B) 秋颱發生時，造成東北部迎風面造成豪大雨，必為共伴效應，與西南氣流無關。

(D) 空氣下沉必造成晴朗天氣。

(E) 題幹已敘述清楚

三、綜合題

<u>36-40 為題組</u>

36. **BD**

【解析】(A) 滲透作用是專指水分子的擴散作用，並非只有活細胞有此現象。

(C) 溶質的擴散不在滲透作用的討論中。

(E) 滲透作用不需要消耗能量。

37. **ACD**

　　【解析】(B) 水分子的淨移動方向爲由細胞內向細胞外。

　　　　　　(E) 液胞有水分的調節的功能，利用水分的進出調節細胞的滲透壓，蔗糖不會隨意進出液胞，物質進出液胞需要有特定的蛋白質幫忙。

38. **BDE**

　　【解析】(A) 氧化能力

　　　　　　(C) 沉澱、凝聚、過濾、曝氣、除臭等

39. **BDE**

　　【解析】(A) pH 值大於 7　　　(C) 使用強酸

40. **D**

　　【解析】$\dfrac{640000 \times \dfrac{0.5}{100}}{320} = 10$ 月，$10 \times 30 = 300$ 天

第貳部分

41. **B**

　　【解析】(A)(D)(E) 選項：熱帶性低壓造成的雲主要以直展雲系爲主，故 (D)(E) 選項錯誤。甲處的雲爲左側熱帶性低壓單獨發展的直展雲，與右側並無關係。

　　　　　　(C) 丙處爲寒潮爆發，表丙處的雲層形成原因爲冷暖空氣接觸的冷鋒造成，並非對流發展旺盛的積雨雲。

42. **A**

　　【解析】此爲記憶性題目；由海水之導電度（電阻倒數，是鹽度與溫度的函數）可計算出鹽度。

43. **C**

【解析】 植物的運動分爲兩種：

(1) 向性，和生長激素分布有關 =＞向光性、向地性等。

(2) 傾性，和膨壓變化有關=>睡眠運動、捕蟲運動、觸發運動等。

選項中 (A) (B) (D) (E) 是由生長素分布不均造成的向性，選項 (C) 睡眠運動是屬於傾性相關運動。

44. **C**

【解析】 根據食物鏈中能量遞減的概念，因能量總量爲乙＞戊＞丁＞甲＞丙，可知食物鏈的順序爲乙⇒戊⇒丁⇒甲⇒丙。乙爲生產者、戊爲初級消費者、丁爲次級消費者、甲爲三級消費者、丙爲最高級消費者。

(A) 甲應爲第四階層。

(B) 乙的個體數是否最多不一定（例如一顆樹上有許多生物）。

(D) 丁不一定是肉食，亦可能爲雜食。

(E) 乙爲生產者。

45. **B**

【解析】 消長是生物群集變化過程，當後起生物替代原先生物後，原先的生物會減少，但並不會瞬間完全消失，彼此會有重疊出現的時空，故答案以 (B) 最佳。

46-47 爲題組

46. **ADE**

【解析】 (B) 此圖天色剛暗表時間大約爲 18:00，故此時台北應

位於下圖中的甲地附近；此時月球仍在地平面上，
表當日月球應位於 B 地。當月球位於 A 地時大約
為農曆二十六日；於 B 地時約為農曆初四。

(C) 木星為類木行星故距離地球較金星遠。

(F) 題幹中敘述往西方低空看去，表照片中的裡面為西
方，此時因在農曆初四，故月球即將西落（參閱下
圖）。

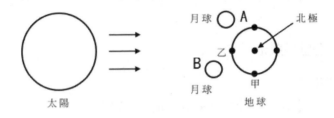

47. **E**

【解析】 因為月球公轉，故一日後月球會公轉至上圖中 B 點右
方 12 度，這造成明日月球晚 50 分鐘升起（地球多自
轉 12 度），故隔日在同一時間觀測月球時，月球的仰
角應比前一日高 12 度左右。金星的公轉週期為 226
日，每日約公轉 1.6 度；木星的公轉週期 4332 日，每
日約公轉 0.01 度；因此隔日的金星與木星的高度與前
一日近似，故選 (E)。

48. **D**

【解析】 (A) 液體：H_2O、Br_2

(B) 氣體：CO_2

(C) SiO_2、MgO、Ca、Si

49. **AC**

【解析】 (B) (D) (E) 含其他元素

50. **E**

【解析】 Cu 活性＞Ag 活性⇒沉澱的是 $Ag_{(s)}$，濾液滴入 $NaCl_{(aq)}$

產生白色沉澱⇒L 仍有 Ag^+

∴L 有 Ag^+、Cu^{2+}、Fe^{2+}

51. **C**

【解析】 $m \times 2 = m \times (-0.5) + 4mv \Rightarrow v = \dfrac{2.5}{4} \approx 0.63(m/s)$

52-53 為題組

52. **E**

【解析】 (A) 火星為行星非地球衛星

(B) 火星太陽之間距離大於日地距離

(C) 火星公轉週期大於地球公轉週期

(D) 晝夜變化與衛星並無關連。

53. **D**

【解析】 令在空中飛 ts，$a = -\dfrac{GM}{r^2}$，初速為 v_0

$v_0 + (-\dfrac{GM}{r^2}) \cdot \dfrac{t}{2} = 0$，$t = \dfrac{2v_0 r^2}{GM} \propto \dfrac{r^2}{M}$

$\dfrac{t_{火}}{t_{地}} = \dfrac{1^2/1}{1.9^2/9.3} = 2.57 \doteqdot 2.6$

54-55 為題組

54. **C**

【解析】 約等於梯形面積 $\dfrac{6(1+2)}{2} = 9$

55. **D**

【解析】 速度 v 與時間 t 圖的斜率爲 a

56. **AD**

【解析】 海溝的三角形表板塊前進並隱沒的方向，故在圖中必爲太平洋板塊隱沒至北美洲板塊之下；此圖爲聚合式板塊邊界，故造成此次地震主要爲逆斷層活動。

57. **A**

【解析】 順向坡的定義爲地表的坡向與岩層的傾斜方向相同，故選 (A)。

58. **DE**

【解析】 人體的專一性防禦可視爲第三層級的防禦作用，需要有 T 淋巴球及 B 淋巴球參與作用。

(A) (B) 爲第一層級的皮膜防禦作用，爲非專一性防禦。

(C) 爲第二層級的發炎反應，爲非專一性防禦。

(D) 和胞毒性 T 細胞的胞殺作用有關，爲專一性防禦。

(E) 和 B 細胞製造抗體有關，爲專一性防禦。

59. **BC**

【解析】 (A) 血管透過微血管來增加和組織間交換物質的面積和效率。

(B) 大腸並無明顯的皺褶式絨毛來增加面積以加速吸收。

(C) 皮膚無吸收或物質交換之必要性。

(D) 肺泡爲氣囊上的突出構造，可以增加氣體交換的表面積。

(E) 小腸的皺褶式絨毛可以增加消化物質的吸收表面積。

60. **CE**

【解析】 (A) 三者都有內皮細胞。

(B) 動、靜脈皆有平滑肌，微血管無。

(D) 動、靜脈皆有結締組織，微血管無。

61. **ABD**

【解析】 (A) 可直接由題目圖中地震之後年分的數據找到。

(B) 地震後該地的族群是由外地移入，所以「再捕捉」個體的比例顯著降低甚至消失。

(C)(D) 地震後的該地的族群是由外地移入，「再捕捉」者為地震前標記而地震後存留下來之個體，從圖可知，之前留下來的個體已顯著降低、甚至消失。

(E) 由圖可知秋冬時並無完全消失。

62-63為題組

62. **AE**

【解析】 (A) 共價鍵 ⇒ Y 是非金屬

(B)(E) 價電子層相差兩層 ⇒ X 是第 2 周期，Y 是第 3 週期（原子序小於 20）

(C) 2

(D) 18

63. **AE**

【解析】 Q_2R

<u>64-65 為題組</u>

64. **AC**

【解析】 (A) (B) 60°C 時，飽和溶液濃度：$\dfrac{100}{100+100} \times 100\% = 50\%$

$\Rightarrow 100g$ 溶液有 $50g$ 溶質

(C) 正確

(D) $\dfrac{50}{100+50} \times 100\% \approx 33.3\%$

(E) 等重量不等莫耳數

65. **AE**

【解析】 (B) 凡得瓦力

(C) 形成離子

(D) (E) $110 \sim 160\,^{\circ}C$ 作用力的屬性相似，$170\,^{\circ}C$ 後劇烈改變

<u>66-67 為題組</u>

66. **DE**

【解析】 (A) (B) 相同　位能=動能 $mgh = \dfrac{1}{2}mv^2 \Rightarrow v = \sqrt{2gh}$ 與質量無關

(C) 重量不同。

67. **CE**

【解析】 力學能守恆

68. **D**

【解析】 由於地層層序由 1 到 5 愈來愈年輕，而地層 1 在上層表地層已經經過倒轉。此種褶皺稱為背斜型向斜。

102 年大學入學學科能力測驗試題
國文考科

第壹部分：選擇題（占 54 分）

一、單選題（占 30 分）

說明：第 1 題至第 15 題，每題有 4 個選項，其中只有一個是正確或
　　　最適當的選項，請畫記在答案卡之「選擇題答案區」。各題
　　　答對者，得 2 分；答錯、未作答或畫記多於一個選項者，該
　　　題以零分計算。

1. 奕軒和同學組隊參加「語文達人競賽」，決勝題抽到的題目是：
　「奴『婢』／麻『痺』／『裨』益，請先判斷『』內三字的讀音
　爲完全相同、完全不同或二同一異，再選出與上述三字發音關係
　相同的一組答案」，正確答案的選項是：
　(A)「劬」勞／「瞿」然／「佝」僂
　(B) 髮「綹」／馬「廄」／自「咎」
　(C) 阿「諛」／舞「雩」／膏「腴」
　(D) 造「詣」／福「祉」／抽「脂」

2. 下列文句「」內成語的運用，正確的選項是：
　(A) 這兩個投機份子「沆瀣一氣」，聯手犯下令人髮指的滔天
　　　罪行
　(B) 前輩苦心孤詣獲致的研究成果，足以作爲我們的「前車之鑑」
　(C) 他畢生致力於改善社會風氣，這種「矯俗干名」的作爲，深
　　　受世人肯定
　(D) 新聞畫面中，落網歹徒個個橫眉豎目、「頭角崢嶸」，讓人
　　　看了不寒而慄

3. 閱讀下文，依序選出最適合填入□□內的選項：

甲、山谷輕輕推開燠熱的晚雲與水氣，適時讓蟬聲鳥聲□□上來，次第溶化在迷幻的暮色。山裡的黃昏，竟不是想像中那樣寧靜。（陳芳明〈辭行山谷〉）

乙、山夜是靜的，螢光一只可謂纖麗，然而繁華盛到極處，流螢稠密已流不動了，住在山裡靜靜的冷光其實變得有聲，那流螢燈火通明照得過了頭，□□裡我開始期待潮平之後的沉幽。（凌拂〈流螢汛起〉）

丙、左邊是平緩柔和的海岸山脈，右邊則是鯉魚山為襯底一路高聳下去的中央山脈。車子在平坦的台九線公路緩緩馳行，突然感覺自己像.翔飛行的鷹，兩旁整齊的山脈宛然雙翼一般□□出一片寶石藍的天空。（王文進〈山脈，雙翼般舒張起來〉）

(A) 浮升／喧嘩／托舉　　　　(B) 飛騰／喧嘩／鼓動
(C) 浮升／明亮／鼓動　　　　(D) 飛騰／明亮／托舉

4. 古漢語中，往往為強調賓語（受詞），而將賓語提到動詞前面。下列不屬於這種語法結構的選項是：

(A) 夫晉，何厭之有
(B) 父母唯其疾之憂
(C) 其一人專心致志，惟弈秋之為聽
(D) 用之則行，舍之則藏，唯我與爾有是夫

5. 下列是一段評論〈擣衣〉詩的文字，依文意選出排列順序最恰當的選項：

〈擣衣〉清而徹，有悲人者。此是
甲、內外相感，愁情結悲　　　乙、秋士悲於心
丙、然後哀怨生焉　　　　　　丁、擣衣感於外
苟無感，何嗟何怨也！（蕭繹《金樓子‧立言篇》）

(A) 乙丙丁甲　　(B) 乙丁甲丙　　(C) 丁甲乙丙　　(D) 丁丙乙甲

6. 右圖是張之洞所撰的蘇軾故居對聯，上下聯各缺兩
   句，請依文意與對聯組成原則，選出甲、乙、丙、
   丁依序最適合填入的選項：

   甲、較量惠州麥飯、儋耳蠻花

   乙、若論東坡八詩、赤壁兩賦

   丙、還是公遊戲文章

   丁、哪得此清幽山水

   右圖對聯：
   五年間謫宦栖遲，〔①〕，〔②〕
   三蘇中天才獨絕，〔③〕，〔④〕

	①	②	③	④
(A)	甲	丁	乙	丙
(B)	乙	丁	甲	丙
(C)	甲	丙	乙	丁
(D)	乙	丙	甲	丁

7. 下列對文人或其著作的敘述，正確的選項是：

   (A) 顧炎武反對空疏之學，重性靈、貴獨創，開清代樸學之風

   (B) 曹雪芹《紅樓夢》，未渲染史傳故事，是清代最出色的諷刺章回小說

   (C) 郁永河《裨海紀遊》透過虛構人物的赴臺採硫，描繪臺灣的地形、氣候、原住民生活等

   (D) 方苞以「學行繼程朱之後，文章在韓歐之間」與友好相期勉，文章嚴標義法，為桐城派初祖

8. 閱讀下列散文詩，選出敘述最恰當的選項：

   中午時候，火一樣的太陽，沒法去遮攔，讓他直曬著長街上。靜悄悄少人行路，只有悠悠風來，吹動路旁楊樹。

   誰家破大門裡，半院子綠茸茸細草，都浮著閃閃的金光。旁邊有一段低低土牆，擋住了個彈三弦的人，卻不能隔斷那三弦鼓盪的聲浪。

　　門外坐著一個穿破衣裳的老年人，雙手抱著頭，他不聲不響。
（沈尹默〈三弦〉）

(A) 畫面描寫由遠而近，逐層推移，旨在表現城鎮之美

(B) 第二節以「綠茸茸細草」、「閃閃的金光」，暗喻三弦樂音
　　的鼓盪

(C) 第三節聚焦於老人的書寫，可看出作者對人間疾苦的觀察

(D) 本詩寫人採畫龍點睛法，點出第三節老人即第二節彈弄三弦
　　的人

9. 閱讀下文，選出敘述正確的選項：

　　起身時，手肘不意擊中了那一疊搖搖欲墜的地圖集，它們乒
乒乓乓摔落地面的粉紅色地磚。十幾巨冊散落三十公分見方磁磚
拼貼出的平面上，攤開的、豎立的、拗折的冊頁在電風扇的吹拂
下搧動，每一頁地圖裡頭的人類都被倒了出來，他們的比例太
小、比重太低，像灰塵一樣散布在我的房間中。（林燿德〈地圖
思考〉）

(A) 藉由擊落地圖集及產生幻象等情境，可見作者的煩躁不安

(B) 散亂一地、姿態各異的地圖集，暗示現實世界的繽紛多彩

(C) 以人類都被倒出來的景象，暗喻國與國之間的界限已經泯除

(D) 關於人類比例的描述，可見作者認為地圖是真實世界的縮影

10. 閱讀下文，選出最切合這段文字核心觀點的選項：

　　我一向認為，生命存在的真假無從辨明，也不重要。重要的
是彼此之間，允許自我「留白」；讓每個人在相互睽視之外，也
可以孤獨地躲進一個任何他者所無法侵入的世界。那也是我們可
以安全地生活一輩子的理由。假如每個人都是「窺夢人」，企圖
窺探他人夢境、窺伺他人內心私密，讓「八卦」入主生活，我不
知道誰能放心地過完這一生。（改寫自顏崑陽〈窺夢人〉）

(A) 假作真時真亦假，真作假時假亦真

(B) 生命存在的真假，無從辨明也無須辨明

(C) 尊重彼此隱私，讓個體能有「留白」空間

(D) 充分防護自我隱私，不讓「八卦」入主生活

11. 閱讀下文，選出最接近本文主旨的選項：

昔有僕嫌其妻之陋者。主翁聞之，召僕至，以銀杯、瓦椀各一，酌酒飲之。問曰：「酒佳乎？」對曰：「佳。」「銀杯者佳乎？瓦椀者佳乎？」對曰：「皆佳。」主翁曰：「杯有精粗，酒無分別。汝既知此，則無嫌於汝妻之陋矣。」僕悟，遂安其室。

（羅大經《鶴林玉露》）
 椀，通碗。

(A) 承恩不在貌

(B) 命無莫強求

(C) 曾經滄海難為水

(D) 糟糠之妻不下堂

12-13為題組

閱讀下文後，回答12-13題。

從前，在巴格達，有個商人派他僕人去市場採購貨物。然而過了片刻，僕人便回來，一臉發白，全身顫抖說：「主人，剛剛在市場，人群中，我被一個女人推了一把。我轉身一看，推我的竟是死神！她直盯著我，並且擺出一個威脅的手勢！現在，把你的馬借我，我要離開這城市，躲過我的命運。我要去撒馬拉。在那裡，死神就不會找到我。」

商人便將馬借他。僕人騎上，立即用馬刺夾緊馬腹，以最快的速度縱馬奔馳而去。後來，這商人也去市場，看見死神站在人群裡，他便走過去，對她說：「今早，你看到我僕人時，為什麼要對他作出威脅的手勢？」「那不是威脅的手勢！」死神答道：「那只是個

吃驚的表示。我只不過看他那時人還在巴格達，大為吃驚。因為，我預定今晚要在撒馬拉和他碰面。」

（毛姆〈撒馬拉之約（Appointment in Samarra）〉，顏靄珠譯）

12. 依據上文，作者描述僕人對死神手勢的理解，其用意是：
(A) 表現人類的生死無常禍福相倚
(B) 反諷僕人的逃避命運弄巧成拙
(C) 強調死神的如影隨形無所不在
(D) 證明主僕的和諧相處共度難關

13. 依據文意，最適合說明僕人心理狀態的選項是：
(A) 心猿意馬　　　　(B) 心蕩神馳
(C) 杯弓蛇影　　　　(D) 捕風捉影

14-15為題組
閱讀下文後，回答14-15題。

　　余居西湖寓樓，樓多鼠，每夕跳踉几案，若行康莊，燭有餘爐，無不見跋。始甚惡之，□□念鼠亦飢耳，至於余衣服書籍一無所損，又何惡焉。適有饋餅餌者，夜則置一枚於案頭以飼之，鼠得餅，不復嚼蠟矣。一夕，余自食餅，覺不佳，復吐出之，遂並以飼鼠。次日視之，餅盡，而余所吐棄者故在。乃笑曰：「鼠子亦狷介乃爾。」是夕，置二餅以謝之。次日，止食其一。余嘆曰：「□□狷介，乃亦有禮。」（俞樾《春在堂隨筆》）

> 跋：火炬或蠟燭燃燒後的殘餘部分。

14. 依據文意，依序選出□□內最適合填入的選項：
(A) 已而／不亦　　　　(B) 俄而／不失
(C) 從而／不無　　　　(D) 繼而／不惟

15. 依據文意,選出敘述錯誤的選項:

(A) 「跳踉几案,若行康莊」,意謂:老鼠橫行無忌,毫不畏懼人

(B) 「燭有餘燼,無不見跋」,意謂:老鼠飢不擇食,連蠟燭都吃

(C) 「余所吐棄者故在」,意謂:老鼠取捨不苟,有所爲有所不爲

(D) 「置二餅以謝之」,意謂:老鼠無損衣物,故得到主人的酬謝

二、多選題(占 24 分)

說明: 第 16 題至第 23 題,每題有 5 個選項,其中至少有一個是正確
的選項,請將正確選項畫記在答案卡之「選擇題答案區」。各
題之選項獨立判定,所有選項均答對者,得 3 分;答錯 1 個選
項者,得 1.8 分;答錯 2 個選項者,得 0.6 分;答錯多於 2 個選
項或所有選項均未作答者,該題以零分計算。

16. 下列文句,完全沒有錯別字的選項是:

(A) 流浪多年,離鄉遊子迫不急待地想要歸返家園

(B) 凡事須依理而爲,委曲求全未必能維持團體和諧

(C) 工作應憑實力獲得敬重,絕不可肆無忌憚仗勢妄爲

(D) 比賽即將結束,衛冕者積分遙遙領先,顯然勝卷在握

(E) 颱風季節將到,防災單位莫不未雨籌謀,預作防範措施

17. 框線內爲某一部《魏晉南北朝
文學史》的目次,依目次選出
對該書敘述正確的選項:

(A) 按照朝代先後次序進行介紹

(B) 詳於詩歌而略於駢文、散文

(C) 對曹氏父子的詩風有所著墨

(D) 強調陶淵明對南朝詩壇的影響

(E) 指出庾信對北朝文風的影響

> 第一章 建安風骨
> 第二章 兩晉詩壇
> 第三章 陶淵明別樹一幟的詩風
> 第四章 謝靈運與詩風的轉變
> 第五章 齊梁詩壇
> 第六章 庾信與南朝文風的北漸
> 第七章 南北朝駢文及散文

18. 下列有關古代文化知識的敘述，正確的選項是：
    (A) 孔門四科為德行、言語、政事、文學
    (B) 古人以二十歲為成年，一般貴族男女，於該年行冠禮
    (C) 諸葛亮〈出師表〉：「先帝創業未半，而中道崩殂。」「崩」，在古代為帝王過世的用語
    (D) 張岱〈西湖七月半〉：「杭人遊湖，巳出酉歸。」「巳出酉歸」，是指：天未亮即出門，傍晚才回家
    (E) 吳敬梓〈范進中舉〉：「范進進學回家，母親、妻子俱各歡喜。」「進學」，是指：范進經「童試」及格，考取秀才

19. 徐志摩〈再別康橋〉：「夏蟲也為我沉默」，句中的「夏蟲」原本只是「無聲」，卻被詩人說成「為我沉默」，是因為詩人把自己的情感投射於夏蟲。下列歌詞，也運用這種手法的選項是：
    (A) 時間是凍結在玄關的雨／模糊你離去的腳印／至少那／漣漪／證明我們曾走在一起
    (B) 淒冷的月暗暝／茫霧罩海邊／海面燈塔白光線／暗淡無元氣／只有是一直發出水螺聲哀悲
    (C) 想我一生的運命／親像風吹打斷線／隨風浮沉沒依偎／這山飄浪過彼山／一旦落土低頭看／只存枝骨身已爛
    (D) 風冷心灰／吻別的季節／每棵樹都在流淚／滿街金黃的落葉／不怪誰／不承認離別／當你搬出我心扉／寂寞翻箱倒櫃
    (E) 今天晚上的／星星很少／不知道它們／跑哪去了／赤裸裸的天空／星星多寂寥／我以為傷心可以很少／我以為我能／過得很好／誰知道一想你／思念苦無藥／無處可逃

20. 敘事文本中，作者有時會運用對話來交代已經發生過的事情，下列引述的對話，具有這種作用的選項是：
    (A) 我怔怔地望著她，想起她美麗的橫愛司髻，我說：「讓我來替你梳個新的式樣吧！」她愀然一笑說：「我還要那樣時髦幹什麼，那是你們年輕人的事了。」

(B) 一個喝酒的人說道：「他怎麼會來？……他打折了腿了。」掌櫃說：「哦！」「他總仍舊是偷。這一回，是自己發昏，竟偷到丁舉人家裡去了。他家的東西，偷得的麼？」「後來怎麼樣？」「怎麼樣？先寫服辯，後來是打，打了大半夜，再打折了腿。」

(C) 「花菜賣多少錢？」巡警問。「大人要的，不用問價，肯要我的東西，就算運氣好。」參說。他就擇幾莖好的，用稻草貫著，恭敬地獻給他。「不，稱稱看！」巡警幾番推辭著說。誠實的參，亦就掛上「稱仔」稱一稱說：「大人，真客氣啦！才一斤十四兩。」

(D) 旁坐有兩人，其一人低聲問那人道：「此想必是白妞了罷？」其一人道：「不是！這人叫黑妞，是白妞的妹子。他的調門兒都是白妞教的，若比白妞，還不曉得差多遠呢！他的好處，人說得出；白妞的好處，人說不出。他的好處，人學得到；白妞的好處，人學不到。」

(E) 停了幾秒鐘，聽到阿旺嫂的聲音：「妳是在說我？」「對！既然說了，也就不怕妳生氣，那段戲最重要，妳怎麼可以離開？」「吉仔撞到木箱子，頭上撞一個大包，哭不停，我哄他，騙他，無效，只好帶他去吃冰！」「難道妳不知道馬上就有妳的戲？」「知道，我怎麼不知道！」「知道還偏偏要去？」

21. 下列各組「」內的文字，前後意義相同的選項是：
(A) 至丹以荊卿為計，始「速」禍焉／況乎視之以至.之勢，重之以疲敝之餘，吏之戕摩剝削以「速」其疾者亦甚矣
(B) 尺寸千里，攢蹙累積，莫得遯隱；縈青繚白，外與天「際」，四望如一／海外獨身遊，風雲「際」會秋。我傳靈德去，仗劍鬼神愁
(C) 臣竊矯君命，以責賜諸民，因燒其券，民稱萬歲，「乃」臣所以為君市義也／公辨其聲，而目不可開，「乃」奮臂以指撥眥，目光如炬

(D) 「比」及三年，可使有勇，且知方也／介而馳，初不甚疾，
　　「比」行百里，始奮迅，自午至酉，猶可二百里，褫鞍甲而
　　不息不汗，若無事然

(E) 有顏回者好學，不遷怒，不貳過。不幸短命死矣，今也則
　　「亡」／家人習奢已久，不能頓儉，必致失所。豈若吾居
　　位、去位、身存、身「亡」，常如一日乎

22. 下列引文，陳述外在環境對人產生影響的選項是：

(A) 居處恭，執事敬，與人忠：雖之夷狄，不可棄也

(B) 善人同處，則日聞嘉訓；惡人從游，則日生邪情

(C) 獨學無友，則孤陋而難成；久處一方，則習染而不自覺

(D) 一齊人傅之，眾楚人咻之，雖日撻而求其齊也，不可得矣

(E) 子欲居九夷。或曰：「陋，如之何？」子曰：「君子居之，
　　何陋之有！」

23. 閱讀下文，選出符合文意的選項：

　　　東蒙山中人喧傳虎來。艾子采茗，從壁上觀。

　　　聞蛇告虎曰：「君出而人民辟易，禽獸奔駭，勢烜赫哉！余
出而免人踐踏，已為厚幸。欲憑藉寵靈，光輝山岳，何道而可？」
虎曰：「憑余軀以行，可耳。」蛇於是憑虎行。

　　　未數里，蛇性不馴。虎被緊纏，負隅聳躍，蛇分二段。蛇怒曰：
「憑得片時，害卻一生，冤哉！」虎曰：「不如是，幾被纏殺！」

　　　艾子曰：「倚勢作威，榮施一時，終獲後災，戒之！」（屠本
畯《艾子外語‧蛇虎告語》）

(A) 艾子世居東蒙山，平日以觀蛇虎相鬥為樂

(B) 憑虎而行的蛇，本性難移，因而對虎不利

(C) 虎置蛇於死地，是因虎性陰狠，事先布局

(D) 本文可用「為虎作倀」形容蛇與虎的關係

(E) 本文旨在告誡世人：藉勢逞威，禍害必至

第貳部分：非選擇題（共三大題，占 54 分）

說明：本部分共有三題，請依各題指示作答，答案必須寫在「答案卷」上，並標明題號一、二、三。作答務必使用筆尖較粗之黑色墨水的筆書寫，且不得使用鉛筆

一、文章解讀（占 9 分）

閱讀框線內文章之後，請以個人想法，評論作者的觀點。文長約 100-150字（約5-7行）。

> 　　世間沒有甚麼一個人必讀之書。因為我們智能上的趣味像一棵樹那樣地生長著，或像河水那樣地流著。只要有適當的樹液，樹便會生長起來，只要泉中有新鮮的泉水湧出來，水便會流著。當水流碰到一個花崗石巖時，它便由巖石的旁邊繞過去；當水流湧到一片低窪的溪谷時，它便在那邊曲曲折折地流著一會兒；當水流湧到一個深山的池塘時，它便恬然停駐在那邊；當水流沖下急流時，它便趕快向前湧去。這麼一來，雖則它沒費甚麼氣力，也沒有一定目標，可是它終究有一天會到達大海。（節錄自林語堂〈讀書的藝術〉）

二、文章分析（占 18 分）

　　閱讀框線內蘇轍〈上樞密韓太尉書〉幾段文字後，回答問題：

（一）綜合材料（甲）與材料（乙），說明蘇轍提及的「養氣方法」有哪些？

（二）就材料（乙）蘇轍的自述，說明材料（甲）與〈上樞密韓太尉書〉的寫作目的有何關聯？

答案必須標明（一）（二）分列書寫。（一）（二）合計文長限 200-250字（約9行-12行）。

材料(甲)：　轍生好爲文，思之至深，以爲文者氣之所形。然文不可以學而能，氣可以養而致。孟子曰：「我善養吾浩然之氣。」今觀其文章，寬厚宏博，充乎天地之間，稱其氣之小大。太史公行天下，周覽四海名山大川，與燕、趙間豪俊交游，故其文疏蕩，頗有奇氣。此二子者，豈嘗執筆學爲如此之文哉？其氣充乎其中而溢乎其貌，動乎其言而見乎其文，而不自知也。　材料(乙)：　且夫人之學也，不志其大，雖多而何爲？轍之來也，於山見終南、嵩、華之高，於水見黃河之大且深，於人見歐陽公，而猶以爲未見太尉也。故願得觀賢人之光耀，聞一言以自壯，然後可以盡天下之大觀而無憾者矣。　轍年少，未能通習吏事。嚮之來，非有取於斗升之祿，偶然得之，非其所樂。然幸得賜歸待選，使得優游數年之間，將歸益治其文，且學爲政。太尉苟以爲可教而辱教之，又幸矣。

三、引導寫作（占 27 分）

曾永義《愉快人間》說：「爲了『人間愉快』，就要『人間處處開心眼』，就要具備擔荷、化解、包容、觀賞等四種能力，達成『蓮花步步生』的境界。」這是一段充滿生命智慧的哲思。「人間愉快」，可以是敞開心胸、放寬眼界的自得；可以是承擔責任、化解問題的喜悅；可以是對周遭事物的諒解和包容；可以是觀照生活情趣的藝術；也可以是……。<u>請根據親身感受或所見所聞，以「**人間愉快**」爲題</u>，寫一篇完整的文章，記敘、抒情、議論皆可，文長不限。

102年度學科能力測驗國文科試題詳解

第壹部分：選擇題

一、單選題

1. **C**

   【解析】 (A) ㄑㄩˊ／ㄐㄩˋ／ㄎㄡˋ

   (B) ㄅㄧㄡˇ／ㄐㄧㄡˋ／ㄐㄧㄡˋ

   (C) ㄩˊ

   (D) ㄧˋ／ㄓˇ／ㄓ

2. **A**

   【解析】 (A) 比喻氣味相投，後多用於貶義。

   (B) 比喻可以作為後人借鏡的失敗經驗或教訓。

   (C) 故意立異違俗以求取名聲。

   (D) 形容才華洋溢，能力出眾的年輕人。

3. **A**

   【解析】 甲：由「輕輕推開」與「次第溶化」可知用較輕柔的
   「浮升」比具力道的「飛騰」合適，且亦符合
   「蟬聲鳥聲」與「晚雲與水氣」對舉的意象。

   乙：「潮平」、「沉幽」為安靜之意，與「喧嘩」對
   比；由「變得有聲」與「照得過了頭」也可知
   為「喧嘩」。

   丙：天空在山脈之上，有擎天之勢，故選「托舉」
   為宜。

4. **D**

【解析】 (A) 有（動）何厭（賓）：哪裡有滿足的時候。

(B) 憂（動）其疾（賓）：擔憂孩子生病。

(C) 聽（動）弈秋（賓）：聽弈秋的講解。

(D) 無倒裝。此處「之」、「是」為代名詞，「之」指（我）孔子；「是」指「用之則行，舍之則藏」的修養。

5. **B**

【解析】 乙、丁是一組，一內一外，然後接甲「內外相感」，「丙」是內外相感的結果。

6. **A**

【解析】 對聯「仄起平收」（上聯末字仄聲，下聯末字平聲），故知 2 為丁，4 為丙。由「還是公遊戲文章」可知前應接蘇軾作品，故 3 為乙。

7. **D**

【解析】 (A) 「重性靈，貴獨創」應為晚明公安派的主張。

(B) 紅樓夢為世情小說。

(C) 為郁永河實際來臺採硫的日記。

8. **C**

【解析】 (A) 由遠而近是對的，但旨在聚焦於孤苦的老人。

(B) 「綠茸茸細草，都浮著閃閃的金光」是因「火一樣的太陽」。

(D) 土牆擋住了彈三弦的人，可見彈三弦的人在門內，而老人在門外，並非同一人。

9. **D**

【解析】 (A) 無煩躁不安,應是引出思考。

(B) 由它們摔落地面的模樣,應是暗示現實世界的紛亂。

(C) 由「比例太小、比重太低,像灰塵一樣」,可知應是描寫人的渺小。

10. **C**

【解析】 由「重要的是彼此之間,允許自我『留白』」與末句對八卦的批判,可知為 (C)。(D)「不讓『八卦』入主生活」是「不窺探他人」而非「充分防護自我隱私」。

11. **A**

【解析】 主人的用意是讓僕人知道,外貌(銀杯、瓦椀)不是重點,重點是內在(酒)。僕人曉悟後便不再嫌棄妻子容貌不佳,安於其室。

(A) 承受恩寵的原因不在於容貌。

(B) 命中註定沒有的不要強求。

(C) 比喻感情方面曾經擁有美好的經驗,如今不能或不願再面對新的對象。

(D) 不能拋棄共患難的妻子。

12-13為題組

12. **B**

【解析】 由後段商人與死神的對話可知,僕人誤解了死神的手勢而赴死,正是逃不脫命運的諷刺。

13. **C**

　　【解析】 (A) 形容心意不定，不能自持。

　　　　　　(B) 形容心神迷亂，不能自持。

　　　　　　(C) 比喻為不存在的事情枉自驚惶。

　　　　　　(D) 比喻所做之事或所說的話毫無根據，憑空揣測。

14-15為題組

14. **D**

　　【解析】 由「始甚惡之」，可知依時間順序敘述，故選「繼而」

　　　　　　（接著）（「已而」、「俄而」是一會兒的意思；「從

　　　　　　而」是因此、因而。）後面空格部分，先笑曰：「鼠

　　　　　　子亦狷介。」再進而言其「有禮」，故知應填「不惟」

　　　　　　（不只）。

15. **D**

　　【解析】 由「次日視之，餅盡，而余所吐棄者故在。乃笑曰：

　　　　　　『鼠子亦狷介乃爾。』是夕，置二餅以謝之。」可知

　　　　　　此餅是向老鼠賠罪的。

二、多選題

16. **BC**

　　【解析】 (A) 迫不「及」待。

　　　　　　(D) 勝「券」在握。

　　　　　　(E) 未雨「綢繆」。

17. **ABCE**

【解析】 (A) 建安→兩晉→陶淵明（晉宋之際）→謝靈運（南朝宋）→齊梁－庾信（梁）。

(B) 前五章言詩，後二章言文。言詩的篇幅較多。

(C) 「建安風骨」的代表作家爲曹操父子與建安七子。

(D) 只說「獨樹一幟」，並未言及影響。

(E) 庾信由南朝入北朝，後留居北朝。且由篇名將二者並列可知庾信將南朝文風帶入北方。

18. **ACE**

【解析】 (B) 男子二十歲成年，行加冠禮；女子十五歲成年，束髮加筓。

(D) 巳：早上九點到十一點；酉：傍晚五點到七點。

19. **BDE**

【解析】 (A) 意謂時間漸漸使我忘記你的離去，並未將感情投射到「時間」。

(B) 月的「凄冷」，燈塔光線的「無元氣」水螺聲的「哀悲」，都是情感的投射。

(C) 譬喻。將命運比擬爲斷線的風箏。

(D) 將落葉看成「樹在流淚」，是情感的投射。

(E) 覺得星星「寂寥」，是情感的投射。

20. **BDE**

【解析】 (A) 對話講的是當下。

(B) 由喝酒的人的對話，得知孔乙己的遭遇（過去的事）。

(C) 對話為買賣的當下。

(D) 由對話得知黑妞從白妞那學藝（過去的事）。

(E) 由對話交代阿旺嫂賴掉一場戲的原因——吉仔撞到頭哭不停（過去的事）。

21. **BD**

【解析】(A) 招致／加速。

(B) 交接。

(C) 是／於是。

(D) 等到。

(E) 無／死亡。

22. **BCD**

【解析】(A) 在家恭敬，做事嚴肅謹慎，待人忠誠：即使到了蠻夷之邦，也不可背棄這些原則。

(B) 和善人再一起，會天天聽到好的道理；和惡人在一起，會日日產生邪惡的思想。

(C) 獨自學習而沒有朋友互相切磋，那麼就會淺薄鄙陋而難有所成；久居於一個地方，就會沾染上該地的習氣而不自覺。

(D) 一個齊人教他齊國話，一群楚人在旁用楚國話吵他，即使天天鞭撻他要求他學好齊國話，也沒辦法啊！

(E) 孔子想要到東夷去住。有人說：「東夷很鄙陋落後啊！怎麼能住？」孔子回答說：「君子住的地方，哪裡會鄙陋落後？」

23. **BE**

【解析】 語譯：

東蒙山中的人喧嚷著老虎來了。艾子上山採茶，旁觀
此事。聽到蛇跟老虎說：「您一出現人民就躲避，禽鳥
百獸駭走奔逃，聲勢真是浩大啊！我要是出現沒被人
踩踏，已經是萬幸了。我想要藉著您的威勢，光耀於
山岳間，怎麼樣才行呢？」老虎說：「你爬上我身上跟
著走，就可以了。」蛇就爬上老虎身上一起走。走沒
幾里路，蛇不安分了。老虎被蛇緊緊纏住，頑強抵抗，
上下跳躍，把蛇斷成兩截。蛇憤怒地說：「只依靠你一
下子，卻葬送了我一條命，真是冤枉啊！」老虎說：
「我不這樣做，差點被你緊纏而死！」艾子說：「仗著
別人的勢力而作威作福，只得一時光榮，最後還是招
致禍害，要引以為戒啊！」

(A) 文中未提及。

(C) 因蛇先對其不利，老虎只是為求脫身。

(D) 為虎作倀：助紂為虐。和本文無關。

第貳部分：非選擇題

（一）作者觀點：

讀書像提供樹生長的適當樹液或者新鮮的源頭活水，只要跟
隨趣味不斷地讀，樹就能生長，水也終有一天匯流至大海。
因此沒有什麼非讀不可的書。

（二）思考：

贊同：要跟著趣味讀書，才能興味盎然、行之久遠。

不贊同：跟著趣味讀書，適合所有人嗎？有沒有前提？符不
符合現實情況？會不會有侷限性？

（三）範例：

在已有一定程度的知識基礎之下，我同意作者的觀點。趣味是引領人主動探索的明燈，依趣味而行，不但得讀書之樂，且易有所成。但如果還在摸索階段，根本不知道知識的大概範疇，有許多未曾接觸過而說不上有沒有興趣的部分，此時即講求「依趣味讀書」，恐怕會像瞎子摸象，抱得象腿就以為是全象，而錯失許多探索的可能。

二、文章分析

（一）蘇轍提到的養氣方法為：

1、效法孟子，修養內在德行；

2、遊歷名山大川，以擴大閱歷；

3、結交豪傑，就教賢士，以砥礪人生境界，壯大心志。

（二）蘇轍寫作＜上樞密韓太尉書＞是為了求見太尉韓琦。一個初出茅廬，年方十九的年輕人，想求見名滿天下的太尉，要讓他願意接見，又不能有諂媚之嫌。所以他從自己學為文下筆，在議論中展現自己的見識：以養氣為經，而鋪陳出遊歷山川、結交豪傑、就教賢士等養氣方法，又以名山大川與歐陽修為緯，襯顯蘇轍對於求見韓琦之渴慕，自然引出求見的主題。

三、引導寫作

【寫作指引】以自身的愉快經歷，利用引導中詮釋的四種切入點，闡述心境，表達所領略、觀察到的人生美景。

【範例】

人間愉快

　　每個月必有一個週日早晨，我頭戴寬邊帽，套上棉布手套，和爸爸、媽媽，社區阿姨、叔伯們，花上一個早晨的時間，給自己帶來好幾天的愉快。

　　我住的社區近郊傍山，舉目是盈滿的綠，充耳皆愉悅的鳥囀。也許因離塵的放鬆與散漫，也許因缺乏管理，社區小徑生長力旺盛的雜草也遮掩不住隨手丟棄的垃圾。而當大家漸漸感覺到在「我見青山多嫵媚」時迴目所及的不協調是多麼尷尬與殺風景，開始有人提議要組個志工隊來整理環境。

　　一開始人丁稀少，只有幾家與發起人交情較好的，友情響應。想想也是，多美好的星期天早晨啊！不在被窩裡多纏綣一會兒，不在雅致的店裡吃頓豐富的早點，多對不起自己啊！但漸漸地，過往的路人好奇於這些「清潔隊」的來歷，忍不住多問幾句後，隊長的掃把如同魔笛般，吸引了越來越多人加入。

　　於是每個月的這天，不能賴床的我，賺了美好的晨光；鄰居活力地招呼著一起出門，彷彿參加一場社區聯誼會；沿著山徑，我們不只掃除垃圾，還青山佳人本色，積累心中多日的壓力、情緒等生活垃圾也被掃蕩一空；當打包好垃圾，上下環視一圈時，當放任活動完、略為疲累的筋骨，癱陷於沙發時——真是愉快啊！

　　能夠在星期天早上，貢獻綿薄之力，與志同道合的夥伴，一起完成這麼有意義的事，使得本來是藍色星期一的前奏曲，反成為活力嘉年華的開場，讓愉快的心境無限延伸。

102 年學測國文科非選擇題閱卷評分原則說明

閱卷召集人：蕭麗華（國立臺灣大學中文系教授）

　　本次參與閱卷的委員，均為各大學中文系、國文系、語文教育系或通識教育中心之教師，共計 231 人，分為 20 組，除正、副召集人統籌所有閱卷事宜外，每組均置一位協同主持人，負責該組閱卷工作，協同主持人均為各大學中文系、國文系之專任教授。

　　1 月 30 日，由正、副召集人與 8 位協同主持人，就 3000 份抽樣之答案卷，詳加評閱、分析、討論，草擬評分原則。每題選出「A」、「B」、「C」等第之標準卷各1份，及試閱卷各 15 份。1 月 31 日，再由正、副召集人與 19 位協同主持人深入討論、評比所選出的標準卷及試閱卷，並審視、修訂所擬之評分原則，確定後，製作閱卷參考手冊，供 2 月 1 日正式閱卷前，各組協同主持人說明及全體閱卷委員參考之用，並作為評分時之參考。

　　本次國文考科非選擇題共三大題，占 54 分。第一大題為文章評論，占 9 分；第二大題為文章分析，占 18 分；第三大題為引導寫作，占 27 分。

　　第一大題要求考生閱讀節錄自林語堂＜讀書的藝術＞中的一段文字後，加以評論。評閱重點，在於檢視考生是否能解讀並評論作者的看法。凡能解讀並評論作者看法，內容充實，理路清晰，文字流暢者，得 A 等（7～9 分）；大致能解讀並評論作者看法，內容平實，文字通順者，得 B 等（4～6 分）；內容貧乏，評論失當，文字蕪雜者，得 C 等（1～3 分）。其次，再視字數是否符合要求，錯別字是否過多，斟酌扣分。

第二大題要求考生閱讀蘇轍＜上樞密韓太尉書＞的兩段文字，分別為 (甲)、(乙) 兩段材料，考生必須綜合這兩段材料回答兩個子題。材料 (甲) 強調為文重在養氣，效法孟子，以修養內在德性；遊歷名山大川，以擴展外在見聞；結交豪俊賢士，以砥礪人生境界，這三者是「養氣的方法」。材料 (乙) 蘇轍自述於「人」已見歐陽公，希望能一見韓琦來壯大自己的心志。兩個子題的問題重心一在蘇轍提及的「養氣的方法」有哪些？一在材料 (甲)、(乙) 與＜上樞密韓太尉書＞的關聯。凡兩個子題皆分析正確深入，文字清暢，敘述清楚者，得 A 等（13～18 分）；兩子題分析欠深入，文字大體平順，或兩子題中只有一個子題分析正確，文字敘述清楚者，得 B 等（7～12分）；兩子題僅部分正確者，得 C 等（1～6 分）。另視是否分列小題作答，字數符合規定與否，及錯別字是否過多，斟酌扣分。

第三大題要求考生根據親身感受或所見所聞，以「人間愉快」為題，寫一篇文章，論說、記敘、抒情皆可，文長不限。評閱重點，從「題旨發揮」、「資料掌握」、「結構安排」、「字句運用」四項指標，加以評分。凡能掌握題幹要求，緊扣題旨發揮，論述周延，富有創意，能深刻回應引導內容，舉證詳實貼切，結構嚴謹，脈絡清楚，字句妥切，邏輯清晰，文筆流暢，修辭優美者，得 A 等（19～27 分）；尚能掌握題幹要求，依照題旨發揮，內容平實，思路尚稱清晰，且尚能回應引導內容，舉證平淡疏略，結構大致完整，脈絡大致清楚，用詞通順，造句平淡，文筆平順，修辭尚可者，得 B 等（10～18 分）；未能掌握題幹要求，題旨不明或偏離題旨，內容浮泛，思路不清，大部分抄襲引導內容，舉證鬆散模糊，結構鬆散，條理紛雜，字句欠當，邏輯不通，文筆蕪蔓，修辭粗俗者，得 C 等（1～9 分）。另視標點符號之使用與錯別字多寡，斟酌扣分。

【附錄一】

102 年度學科能力測驗
英文考科公佈答案

題號	答案	題號	答案	題號	答案
1	B	21	D	41	A
2	C	22	A	42	A
3	A	23	B	43	D
4	D	24	C	44	C
5	C	25	C	45	D
6	B	26	B	46	C
7	A	27	A	47	D
8	D	28	B	48	B
9	B	29	A	49	A
10	C	30	D	50	B
11	C	31	D	51	C
12	D	32	I	52	D
13	A	33	E	53	B
14	D	34	C	54	C
15	C	35	B	55	D
16	B	36	J	56	B
17	D	37	A		
18	D	38	F		
19	B	39	G		
20	A	40	H		

102 年度學科能力測驗
國文、數學考科公佈答案

國　文		數　學				
題號	答案	題號	答案	題　號		答案
1	C	1	5	A	13	1
2	A	2	4		14	6
3	A	3	3		15	－
4	D	4	5	B	16	4
5	B	5	2		17	1
6	A	6	3		18	2
7	D	7	1,2,3,5	C	19	1
8	C	8	1,2		20	9
9	D	9	4,5		21	－
10	C	10	1,3,4	D	22	2
11	A	11	1,2,5		23	7
12	B	12	1,3		24	0
13	C			E	25	5
14	D				26	1
15	D			F	27	3
16	BC				28	1
17	ABCE			G	29	4
18	ACE				30	1
19	BDE				31	5
20	BDE			H	32	1
21	BD				33	5
22	BCD				34	1
23	BE				35	1

102 年度學科能力測驗
社會考科公佈答案

題號	答案	題號	答案	題號	答案	題號	答案
1	D	21	D	41	C	61	D
2	C	22	A	42	D	62	C
3	A	23	B	43	D	63	D
4	B	24	C	44	C	64	A
5	C	25	A	45	A	65	D 或 C
6	D	26	A	46	C	66	D
7	C	27	B	47	A	67	A
8	B	28	A	48	A	68	C
9	C	29	D	49	D	69	A
10	B	30	B	50	A	70	B
11	D	31	C	51	C	71	C
12	A	32	C	52	D	72	D
13	B	33	C	53	C		
14	C	34	D	54	B		
15	D	35	D 或 A	55	B		
16	D	36	B	56	B		
17	A	37	B	57	A		
18	C	38	C	58	B		
19	A 或 C	39	D	59	A		
20	A	40	B	60	D		

102年度學科能力測驗
自然考科公佈答案

題號	答案	題號	答案	題號	答案	題號	答案
1	D 或 B	21	E	41	B	61	ABD
2	C	22	C	42	A	62	AE
3	B	23	D	43	C	63	AE
4	B	24	A	44	C	64	AC
5	C	25	B	45	B	65	AE
6	A	26	D	46	ADE	66	DE
7	C	27	CE	47	E	67	CE
8	D	28	AE	48	D	68	D
9	D	29	CEF	49	AC		
10	A	30	CDE	50	E		
11	A	31	ABE	51	C		
12	C	32	AC	52	E		
13	E	33	CDE	53	D		
14	D	34	CD	54	C		
15	D	35	AC	55	D		
16	A	36	BD	56	AD		
17	E	37	ACD	57	A		
18	A	38	BDE	58	DE		
19	E	39	BDE	59	BC		
20	D	40	D	60	CE		

【附錄二】

102 年度學科能力測驗
總級分與各科成績標準一覽表

項目＼標準	頂標	前標	均標	後標	底標
國　文	13	12	11	9	7
英　文	14	13	10	6	4
數　學	12	10	7	4	3
社　會	14	13	11	9	7
自　然	13	11	9	6	5
總級分	63	57	47	36	27

※五項標準之計算，均不含缺考生（總級分之計算不含五科都缺考的考生）之成績，計算方式如下：

　　頂標：成績位於第 88 百分位數之考生級分。

　　前標：成績位於第 75 百分位數之考生級分。

　　均標：成績位於第 50 百分位數之考生級分。

　　後標：成績位於第 25 百分位數之考生級分。

　　底標：成績位於第 12 百分位數之考生級分。

【附錄三】

102年度學科能力測驗
各科級分人數百分比累計表

	級分	人　數	百分比（%）	累計人數	累計百分比（%）
國	15	3,777	2.55	148,060	100.00
	14	9,920	6.70	144,283	97.45
	13	19,029	12.85	134,363	90.75
	12	24,155	16.31	115,334	77.90
	11	22,911	15.47	91,179	61.58
	10	18,733	12.65	68,268	46.11
	9	14,653	9.90	49,535	33.46
	8	11,068	7.48	34,882	23.56
	7	8,446	5.70	23,814	16.08
	6	6,120	4.13	15,368	10.38
文	5	4,297	2.90	9,248	6.25
	4	2,731	1.84	4,951	3.34
	3	1,581	1.07	2,220	1.50
	2	574	0.39	639	0.43
	1	63	0.04	65	0.04
	0	2	0.00	2	0.00
英	15	7,713	5.22	147,750	100.00
	14	13,606	9.21	140,037	94.78
	13	16,781	11.36	126,431	85.57
	12	15,194	10.28	109,650	74.21
	11	12,201	8.26	94,456	63.93
	10	11,417	7.73	82,255	55.67
	9	10,288	6.96	70,838	47.94
	8	8,864	6.00	60,550	40.98
	7	9,398	6.36	51,686	34.98
	6	8,463	5.73	42,288	28.62
文	5	9,626	6.52	33,825	22.89
	4	12,001	8.12	24,199	16.38
	3	10,002	6.77	12,198	8.26
	2	2,122	1.44	2,196	1.49
	1	66	0.04	74	0.05
	0	8	0.01	8	0.01

	級分	人　數	百分比（%）	累計人數	累計百分比（%）
數	15	2,881	1.95	147,985	100.00
	14	3,569	2.41	145,104	98.05
	13	4,687	3.17	141,535	95.64
	12	7,641	5.16	136,848	92.47
	11	8,410	5.68	129,207	87.31
	10	12,334	8.33	120,797	81.63
	9	12,270	8.29	108,463	73.29
	8	15,857	10.72	96,193	65.00
	7	13,527	9.14	80,336	54.29
	6	13,324	9.00	66,809	45.15
學	5	14,253	9.63	53,485	36.14
	4	11,716	7.92	39,232	26.51
	3	14,222	9.61	27,516	18.59
	2	9,683	6.54	13,294	8.98
	1	3,504	2.37	3,611	2.44
	0	107	0.07	107	0.07
社	15	5,054	3.42	147,935	100.00
	14	15,181	10.26	142,881	96.58
	13	18,228	12.32	127,700	86.32
	12	25,888	17.50	109,472	74.00
	11	19,595	13.25	83,584	56.50
	10	20,216	13.67	63,989	43.25
	9	12,274	8.30	43,773	29.59
	8	10,222	6.91	31,499	21.29
	7	10,785	7.29	21,277	14.38
	6	6,174	4.17	10,492	7.09
會	5	3,621	2.45	4,318	2.92
	4	618	0.42	697	0.47
	3	71	0.05	79	0.05
	2	5	0.00	8	0.01
	1	2	0.00	3	0.00
	0	1	0.00	1	0.00

級分	人　數	百分比 (%)	累計人數	累計百分比 (%)
15	4,566	3.09	147,643	100.00
14	6,997	4.74	143,077	96.91
13	9,473	6.42	136,080	92.17
12	11,662	7.90	126,607	85.75
11	13,521	9.16	114,945	77.85
10	14,864	10.07	101,424	68.70
9	15,384	10.42	86,560	58.63
8	15,116	10.24	71,176	48.21
7	14,927	10.11	56,060	37.97
6	14,741	9.98	41,133	27.86
5	14,790	10.02	26,392	17.88
4	9,099	6.16	11,602	7.86
3	2,259	1.53	2,503	1.70
2	221	0.15	244	0.17
1	17	0.01	23	0.02
0	6	0.00	6	0.00

（自然）

【劉毅老師的話】

　　我們出版歷屆的學測或指考試題詳解時，都會附上許多相關統計表格。不要小看這些表格，它們能讓你了解競爭者的實力，好勉勵自己要精益求精。

【附錄四】

102 年度學科能力測驗
總級分人數百分比累計表

總級分	人數	百分比	累計人數	累計百分比
75	163	0.11	148,208	100.00
74	363	0.24	148,045	99.89
73	576	0.39	147,682	99.65
72	711	0.48	147,106	99.26
71	934	0.63	146,395	98.78
70	1,200	0.81	145,461	98.15
69	1,395	0.94	144,261	97.34
68	1,664	1.12	142,866	96.40
67	1,858	1.25	141,202	95.27
66	2,040	1.38	139,344	94.02
65	2,245	1.51	137,304	92.64
64	2,531	1.71	135,059	91.13
63	2,707	1.83	132,528	89.42
62	2,783	1.88	129,821	87.59
61	3,062	2.07	127,038	85.72
60	3,171	2.14	123,976	83.65
59	3,350	2.26	120,805	81.51
58	3,519	2.37	117,455	79.25
57	3,714	2.51	113,936	76.88
56	3,874	2.61	110,222	74.37
55	3,932	2.65	106,348	71.76
54	3,935	2.66	102,416	69.10
53	4,026	2.72	98,481	66.45
52	3,844	2.59	94,455	63.73
51	3,933	2.65	90,611	61.14
50	3,902	2.63	86,678	58.48
49	3,980	2.69	82,776	55.85
48	3,909	2.64	78,796	53.17
47	3,782	2.55	74,887	50.53
46	3,760	2.54	71,105	47.98
45	3,628	2.45	67,345	45.44
44	3,732	2.52	63,717	42.99
43	3,499	2.36	59,985	40.47
42	3,364	2.27	56,486	38.11
41	3,260	2.20	53,122	35.84
40	3,060	2.06	49,862	33.64

總級分	人數	百分比	累計人數	累計百分比
39	2,817	1.90	46,802	31.58
38	2,704	1.82	43,985	29.68
37	2,736	1.85	41,281	27.85
36	2,544	1.72	38,545	26.01
35	2,401	1.62	36,001	24.29
34	2,264	1.53	33,600	22.67
33	2,137	1.44	31,336	21.14
32	2,097	1.41	29,199	19.70
31	2,069	1.40	27,102	18.29
30	1,994	1.35	25,033	16.89
29	2,120	1.43	23,039	15.55
28	2,003	1.35	20,919	14.11
27	2,110	1.42	18,916	12.76
26	2,095	1.41	16,806	11.34
25	2,181	1.47	14,711	9.93
24	2,050	1.38	12,530	8.45
23	1,917	1.29	10,480	7.07
22	1,936	1.31	8,563	5.78
21	1,679	1.13	6,627	4.47
20	1,402	0.95	4,948	3.34
19	1,093	0.74	3,546	2.39
18	819	0.55	2,453	1.66
17	565	0.38	1,634	1.10
16	349	0.24	1,069	0.72
15	210	0.14	720	0.49
14	128	0.09	510	0.34
13	67	0.05	382	0.26
12	44	0.03	315	0.21
11	36	0.02	271	0.18
10	34	0.02	235	0.16
9	30	0.02	201	0.14
8	24	0.02	171	0.12
7	28	0.02	147	0.10
6	25	0.02	119	0.08
5	27	0.02	94	0.06
4	26	0.02	67	0.05
3	28	0.02	41	0.03
2	12	0.01	13	0.01
1	0	0.00	1	0.00
0	1	0.00	1	0.00

註：累計百分比＝從0到該級分的累計人數／（報名人數－五科均缺考人數）

【附錄五】

102 年度學科能力測驗
原始分數與級分對照表

科目	國 文	英 文	數 學	社 會	自 然
級距	5.90	6.31	6.42	8.86	8.16
級分	分　數　區　間				
15	82.61 - 108.00	88.35 - 100.00	89.89 - 100.00	124.05 - 144.00	114.25 - 128.00
14	76.71 - 82.60	82.04 - 88.34	83.47 - 89.88	115.19 - 124.04	106.09 - 114.24
13	70.81 - 76.70	75.73 - 82.03	77.05 - 83.46	106.33 - 115.18	97.93 - 106.08
12	64.91 - 70.80	69.42 - 75.72	70.63 - 77.04	97.47 - 106.32	89.77 - 97.92
11	59.01 - 64.90	63.11 - 69.41	64.21 - 70.62	88.61 - 97.46	81.61 - 89.76
10	53.11 - 59.00	56.80 - 63.10	57.79 - 64.20	79.75 - 88.60	73.45 - 81.60
9	47.21 - 53.10	50.49 - 56.79	51.37 - 57.78	70.89 - 79.74	65.29 - 73.44
8	41.31 - 47.20	44.18 - 50.48	44.95 - 51.36	62.03 - 70.88	57.13 - 65.28
7	35.41 - 41.30	37.87 - 44.17	38.53 - 44.94	53.17 - 62.02	48.97 - 57.12
6	29.51 - 35.40	31.56 - 37.86	32.11 - 38.52	44.31 - 53.16	40.81 - 48.96
5	23.61 - 29.50	25.25 - 31.55	25.69 - 32.10	35.45 - 44.30	32.65 - 40.80
4	17.71 - 23.60	18.94 - 25.24	19.27 - 25.68	26.59 - 35.44	24.49 - 32.64
3	11.81 - 17.70	12.63 - 18.93	12.85 - 19.26	17.73 - 26.58	16.33 - 24.48
2	5.91 - 11.80	6.32 - 12.62	6.43 - 12.84	8.87 - 17.72	8.17 - 16.32
1	0.01 - 5.90	0.01 - 6.31	0.01 - 6.42	0.01 - 8.86	0.01 - 8.16
0	0.00 - 0.00	0.00 - 0.00	0.00 - 0.00	0.00 - 0.00	0.00 - 0.00

級分計算方式如下：

1. 級距：以各科到考考生，計算其原始得分前百分之一考生（取整數，小數無條件進位）的平均原始得分，再除以 15，並取至小數第二位，第三位四捨五入。

2. 本測驗之成績採級分制，原始得分 0 分為 0 級分，最高為 15 級分，缺考以 0 級分計。各級分與原始得分、級距之計算方式詳見簡章第 9~10 頁。

102 年學科能力測驗各科試題詳解

主　　　編 / 劉　毅		
發　行　所 / 學習出版有限公司	☎ (02) 2704-5525
郵　撥　帳　號 / 0512727-2 學習出版社帳戶	
登　記　證 / 局版台業 *2179* 號	
印　刷　所 / 裕強彩色印刷有限公司	
台　北　門　市 / 台北市許昌街 10 號 2 F	☎ (02) 2331-4060
台灣總經銷 / 紅螞蟻圖書有限公司	☎ (02) 2795-3656
美國總經銷 / Evergreen Book Store	☎ (818) 2813622
本公司網址　www.learnbook.com.tw	
電　子　郵　件　learnbook@learnbook.com.tw	

售價：新台幣二百二十元正

2013 年 5 月 1 日初版

ISBN 978-986-231-198-1